T·H·E
NETWORKING
B·O·O·K

Decide to Network

Decide to network
Use every letter you write
Every conversation you have
Every meeting you attend
To express your fundamental beliefs and dreams
Affirm to others the vision of the world you want
Network through thought
Network through action
Network through love
Network through the spirit
You are the center of a network
You are the center of the world
You are a free, immensely powerful source
of life and goodness
Affirm it
Spread it
Radiate it
Think day and night about it
And you will see a miracle happen:
the greatness of your own life.
In a world of big powers, media, and monopolies
But of four and a half billion individuals
Networking is the new freedom
the new democracy
a new form of happiness.

Robert Muller

The Authors

Jessica Lipnack and Jeffrey Stamps are founders and directors of the Networking Institute, Inc., Waltham, Massachusetts, publishers of the *Networking Newsletter* and *Networking Journal*. They hold executive positions with Internetwork Communications Inc., which offers electronic networking services. They are married, and are the parents of two daughters, Miranda and Eliza.

T·H·E
NETWORKING
B·O·O·K

PEOPLE CONNECTING WITH PEOPLE

**JESSICA LIPNACK
AND JEFFREY STAMPS**

Jessica Lipnack

Jeffrey Stamps

ROUTLEDGE & KEGAN PAUL
NEW YORK AND LONDON

Joanna and Gary Gruber 1-87

First published in 1986 by
Routledge & Kegan Paul Inc.
in association with Methuen Inc.
29 West 35th Street, New York, NY 10001

Published in the UK by
Routledge & Kegan Paul plc
11 New Fetter Lane, London EC4P 4EE

Phototypeset in Linotron Sabon 10 on 12pt
by Input Typesetting Ltd, London
and printed in Great Britain
by The Guernsey Press Co Ltd
Guernsey, Channel Islands

Library of Congress Cataloging in Publication Data

Lipnack, Jessica.
The networking book.

1. Associations, institutions, etc.—United States.
2. Self-help groups—United States.   3. Associations,
institutions, etc.—United States—Directories.
4. Self-help groups—United States—Directories.
I. Stamps, Jeffrey.   II. Title.
AS29.5.L55 1986   061'.3   86–6566

British Library CIP Data also available
ISBN 0–7102–0976–2

to
Miranda and Eliza

Contents

Foreword

by R. Buckminster Fuller

The world-integrating networking self-multiplies and accelerates. Never ever traveling as a tourist, I myself have been induced into forty-eight complete encirclements of our planet and everywhere I go I meet more and more people whom I had met elsewhere. Ever more widely traveling, literate, well-informed individuals discover that they, and an ever-faster increasing number of other humans, are becoming intuitively aware that life is breaking them out of the ages-long anonymous life patterning of the beehive drone. They experience newborn hope that humans have indeed a destiny of individual significance complementary to the integrity of other individuals.

The networking accelerates as does light in Einstein's equation $E = Mc^2$. The lower case c is the symbol for the linear speed of light, 186,000 miles per second. When not reflectively focused, light expands omniradially as a sphere growing in any one direction at 186,000 miles per second. The rate of surface growth of a spherical wave system is always the second power of the linear growth. That is why it is c^2 in Einstein's equation, which means $186,000 \times 186,000$ miles of surface growth per second. So it is with thought which travels outwardly in all directions to internetwork the people of our 8,000-mile-diameter spherical space home.

As the networking accelerates humanity into a spherically embracing, spontaneous union, yesterday's locally autonomous, self-preoccupied governments will find that trying to arrest networking is like trying to arrest the waves of the ocean.

Spaceship Earth now has 150 admirals. The five admirals in the staterooms immediately above the ship's fuel tanks claim that they "own" the oil. The admirals with staterooms surrounding the ship's

ix

kitchen, dining rooms and food refrigerators claim they own all the food. Those with a stateroom next to a lifeboat claim that they own the lifeboat and so forth. They then have a ship's game called balance of trade. Very soon the majority of admirals have a deficit balance. All the while, the starboard-side admirals are secretly planning to list the boat to port so far as to drown the portside admirals, while the portside admirals are secretly trying to list the boat to starboard so badly as to drown the starboard-side admirals. Nobody is paying any attention to operating the ship or steering it to some port. They run out of food and fuel. They discover that they can no longer reach a port of supply. Finis.

Humanity is now experiencing history's most difficult evolutionary transformation. We are changing from a 95 percent illiterate and rooted lifestyle. We are almost unconsciously drifting away from self-identity with our for-ages-long-physically-remote-from-one-another existence as 150 separate, sovereign nations. Now the uprooted humans of all nations are spontaneously deploying into their physically integrated highways-airways, satellite-relayed world-around telephone speakways and big-city way-stationed world living system.

We may soon be atom-bombed into extinction by the pre-emptive folly of the exclusively for money-making supranational corporations' weaponry industry's political puppet administrators of the now hopelessly bankrupt greatest weapons-manufacturing nations.

If not bomb-terminated we are on our ever-swifter way to becoming an omni-integrated, majorly literate, unified Spaceship Earth society.

The new human *networks* emergence represents the natural evolutionary expansion into the just completed, thirty-years-in-its-building, world-embracing, physical communications network. The new reorienting of human "networking" constitutes the heart and mind pumped flow of life and intellect into the world arteries.

Preface

This book wants to be in print.

In October 1979, we began our research on networks and networking by writing a short letter to one person in rural Alabama. Robert A. Smith, III, responded, sending us the names of nine people interested in networking.

We wrote to them, and they to us, referring us on to more people. By the time we finished the original research, we'd received the names of roughly 50,000 people and organizations around the world, from village councils to multinational corporations.

We wrote to 4,000 of them; 1,500 answered, and those were the people we wrote about in *Networking: The First Report and Directory*, published by Doubleday & Company in April 1982.

We continued to hear from networkers. At the end of that year, we incorporated The Networking Institute to publish information and develop tools for networking—a newsletter, journal, membership directory, and mailing list.

In 1985, we started to develop computer networking systems—using computers and telecommunications to help people connect with people—including the regional New England Commons and the larger-scale International Commons.

One of the people whom we contacted early in our network research is Yoneji Masuda, the Japanese computer visionary, author of many books, and an advocate of networking through telecommunications. In 1984, under the guidance of Mr Masuda, the text of the first edition of *Networking* was published in Japan by President-sha, having been translated by the Japanese government.

The lively Japanese interest in networking is a harbinger for the rest of the world. While the theme of our original book was

"Another America," the theme of this book is the "Invisible Planet ." Networks around the globe connect people.

Eileen Wood Campbell, an editor at Routledge & Kegan Paul in London, encouraged us to revise the original text of the book, and republish it with her company.

What appears here includes many pieces that we have written for Networking Institute publications during the past several years. When it came time to revise the 1982 book, we realized that we had simply continued to "write" the revision manuscript since the book's first publication.

And that process continues.

Acknowledgments

Thousands of people have helped this book along, beginning with the very first people we wrote to for information in 1979, and continuing through the members of The Networking Institute. Thank you, one and all, for your thoughtfulness and inspiration as world-class networkers.

For this edition, we are particularly grateful to R. Buckminster Fuller, who wrote the Foreword in 1982, just as the original book was going to press, a little more than a year before the death of him and his wife Anne. It was too late to add Bucky's contribution to that book, and we held it, with the hope that there would be another edition. Many thanks, Bucky.

And, we are grateful to Robert Muller, who wrote the poem on the first page of this book. Robert's poem just arrived as a gift through the mail one day. Our original interview with Robert in 1980 had profoundly deepened our understanding of networking, and we are honored that this book will carry his poem around the world.

We would not know Robert Muller, or thousands of other people, were it not for Robert A. Smith, III, our friend for many years now. Bob set up the initial set of connections that has led to the work we are doing now.

Yoneji Masuda, responsible for the publication of our book in Japan, is another to whom Bob Smith led us. This English edition of the book allows us to thank Mr Masuda in print and in public for his critical contribution to the development of global networking.

The logo on the cover of this book is another gift that simply came through the mail. Just as we were starting The Networking Institute (known as TNI), we received a sketch of this networking "mark" from J. Gordon Lippincott, who has designed logos for many of the world's largest corporations. In his final design, Gordon bent the connecting lines into the arcs that give the logo its "global" feel, and we thought it belonged on the cover of this Invisible Planet book.

We know Virginia Hine would agree with us. Ginnie, as she was known to her friends, helped us considerably with the original edition. We feel extremely fortunate to have become friends with her before she died in 1982, and we feel her inspiration still.

Ron Bernstein, our literary agent, has seen our work develop from a four-page book proposal to now this edition, and we appreciate his continuing advice.

There would be no new publication were it not for Eileen Wood Campbell who perceived the need and created the opportunity for this book. A bow in your direction, Eileen. And we are grateful for the encouragement and effort of Marion Russell.

Since the time we started TNI, the staff and projects have grown from just the two of us to many. Three people who helped immeasurably with this edition: Jean Sullivan, Linda Ottavi and John Boynton. Thank you, you three, for the many ways in which you've contributed to this process, many times late into the night. We also appreciate Dianne Brause's contribution as the first person to join our work at TNI.

We've benefited from the support of Bob and Suellen McAndrews, who made their maiden voyage to visit us in West Newton just as we began our research in 1979. That they are now neighbors, and that Bob is now our business partner, makes us happy indeed.

Through Bob's involvement here, we were able to launch our computer networking enterprise, but not without the help of Bill Johnson of Digital Equipment Corporation. Keep the faith, B.J.

Larry Brilliant and Ron Weiser have helped us shape an idea into a real business, practicing the best of networking principles as they go. We feel blessed to have met you, Larry and Ron.

June Mullen has been a mainstay in our daily support, coming and going since the early days of our research, making numerous trips to the printer, and generally caring for our family in ways one would expect from a much older person.

Our friends at Roberts Printing, Tom Larson, Frieda Campbell and Gary Walsh, who have printed everything we've published at The Networking Institute, including the periodicals in which much of the material included here first appeared, deserve more credit than acknowledgments provide.

So do other friends and colleagues who have encouraged and supported our work again and again: Tom Hargadon, Jimmy and Holly Morris, Lucrecy Johnson, Mirtala, Lisa Woody, Emily and Tom LaMont, Judy Smith and Robb Burlage, Priscilla Harmel and Alan Shapiro, Kate and Ben Taylor, Ron Blau and Judy Levin, Angela Smith, Phil Collier, Stan Pokras, Christine Siegrist, Frank Catanzaro, Gerald McDade (senior and junior), Bill Ellis, Richard North, Bill Reckmeyer, Pat Wagner and Leif Smith, Darrell Icenogle, Eric Williams, Kim Lanzillotta, Anne Marie McDonald, Jody Tamis, Bob Mueller, and Peter Russell.

One friend, also a colleague of several years now, has enabled us to see what a miracle networking can be: Sandra Grear. The early and continuing support of Mark Horowitz and Abby Seixas is also much appreciated.

Our relatives have been our friends too: Ann Stamps, Ethel Lipnack, Eric Lipnack, David Stamps and Susan Stamps.

Finally, we have our children, Eliza and Miranda, to thank as well. Precious girls, we love you. You give us strength and understanding.

Jessica Lipnack
Jeffrey Stamps

West Newton, Massachusetts
December 1985

CHAPTER 1

Discovering networking

When historians of the future reflect on this time, they may discover that some of our era's most significant inventions have been social, not technological. Germinated in the uproar of the 1960s and born in the self-reflection of the 1970s, networks appear to be coalescing everywhere in the 1980s, an appropriate-sociology response to bureaucratic logjams. As potent and poignant antidotes to loneliness and fragmentation, networks link people of like minds, be they secondary school administrators in Minnesota, agronomists in Asia or doctors everywhere working to prevent nuclear war.

We hear the word "network" every day. A television network. A telephone network. Networks of pathways, roadways, railways and waterways. Or simply *Network*, the Hollywood film, remembered for the TV commentator shouting, "I'm mad as hell and I'm not going to take it any more."

The word has come to describe all types of people associations: a friendship network, a neighborhood network, a women's network, a board member network, a self-help network, an old-boy network, a scuba-diving network, a knitters' network.

Seymour Sarason, a sociologist at Yale University, writes extensively about "human resource networks." Psychologists Ross Speck and Carolyn Attneave have developed a psychotherapeutic model called "network therapy." The academic discipline of social network analysis publishes a scholarly journal called *Social Networks*.

The *Oxford Universal Dictionary* cites the first use of the word in 1560, meaning "a work in which threads, wires, or the like are arranged in the form of a net," or later "a complex structure of rivers, canals, railways, or wireless transmitting stations."

A network in the modern sense, in the sense we use it in this

1

book, has no dictionary definition ... yet. The word itself has evolved not as jargon, but to mean something new, something that can be regarded as being similar to, yet quite different from, its earlier meanings. Its more complex usage extends the word into additional grammatical forms. The noun is "a network." The verb is "to network." The gerund is "networking." A person who networks is a "networker." The word even crosses language barriers. In Japan, the word for networking is "networking," transliterated into Japanese characters.

This new meaning of "network" includes but is not limited to these images:

- a physical system that looks like a tree or a grid;
- a system of nodes and links;
- a map of lines between points;
- a persisting identity of relationships;
- a "badly knotted fishnet";
- a structure that knows no bounds;
- a nongeographic community;
- a support system;
- a lifeline;
- everybody you know;
- everybody you know who ... swims, collects coins, sings in the church choir, watches the children walk to school, reads Teilhard de Chardin. . . .

What is a network?

What is a network? A network is a web of free-standing participants cohering through shared values and interests. Networks are composed of self-reliant people and of independent groups.

What is networking? Networking is people connecting with people, linking ideas and resources. Networking has entered the lexicon to mean *making connections among peers.* One person with a need contacts another with a resource, and networking begins.

The rise of networks is accompanying other cultural shifts. Future forecaster John Naisbitt cites the shift from hierarchy to networks as one of ten major *megatrends* shaping the future. "We are giving up dependence on hierarchical structures in favor of informal networks," he writes. Whereas once charts of pyramiding boxes were believed to be the only rational map by which people organize themselves, today systems of intertwining, densely populated networks can be found supplementing, weaving through, and sometimes entirely eclipsing bureaucracies.

Though personal networking is as old as the human story, only in the past few decades have people consciously used it as an organizational tool and only now are people beginning to put a name to it. While classic "old boy" networks have held things in check for centuries with their limited view of the meaning of "we," in recent years networking has opened up new lines of communication, both locally and globally.

A few examples give the broad scope of networking and its humble elegance:

- In remote Rangeley, Maine, Bill Ellis, a physicist and advisor to international agencies, tends TRANET (Transnational Appropriate/Alternative Technology Network) with participants on five continents, by publishing a quarterly newsletter and answering thousands of information requests each year. Ellis says it's easier to network from this tiny village near the Canadian border than it would be in New York.
- In Tokyo, Masaaki Shiihara, a veteran Vietnam War journalist, invites just over 100 colleagues to form Networking 108, a tight web of professionals who share ideas and resources at monthly meetings.
- In Boston, Massachusetts, an independent jewelry saleswoman, concerned about the lack of connections among her female colleagues and cognizant of the industry's men-only associations such as New York's 24–Carat Club, invites seventy-five women to get together and nearly fifty show up. New England Women in the Jewelry Industry is born, providing the women, previously isolated in their individual jobs, with a place to meet and share concerns.
- In Bogota, Colombia, a Boeing 707 jet lands, carrying medicine, tents, canned foods and clothing for the survivors of the mud slide that submerged two villages at the base of a volcano. Rodrigo Arboleda Halaby, an international networker, has filled

the plane simply by letting his friends and associates know of the need.

- In Denver, Colorado, the Office for Open Network of Pattern Research organizes an information file that allows people to find others—whether investor and inventor or tenderfoot and trail guide. Leif Smith and Patricia Wagner are the network's "weavers."

In addition to linking up people with complementary needs and resources, networking is also used as a conscious alternative to top-down organization. In Newark, Delaware, W. L. Gore and Associates, manufacturers of Gore-tex, a water-resistant fabric that "breathes," operate a multimillion-dollar corporation with a networking management structure that founder Bill Gore calls the "lattice." People are grouped around projects; projects are undertaken on the basis of commitment. The firm's 2,000 "associates," not employees, have not bosses but "sponsors."

Nowhere is the use of the words *network* and *networking* more prevalent than in the computer world: the large centralized behemoths that ruled the electronic world of only a few years past are now encircled by decentralized nets of small autonomous microcomputers.

A computer network is a web of free-standing computers linked by shared electronic protocols. At the leading edge of social change, people working at home in Toffler's *Third Wave* "electronic cottages" are by definition free-standing. When people interact from their electronic cottages and from their personal computers at work, they do so as self-reliant participants in a larger network. Their electronic connections, for all the suggestive Orwellian imagery, are potentially equal. With the technology in high-speed flux, every new link is forged on the frontier, where cooperation is more socially adaptive than competition.

In the end, it is this sense of cooperation among self-reliant, decision-making peers that vitalizes a network. Networking swallows up buck passing and renders each of us more responsible, self-respecting and creative. The process of networking itself changes those who are networked, by expanding each person's matrix of connections.

4

Networks as organization

Until the past several decades, network theory was drawn from the physical world. Road, telephone and television networks, with their entrances, byways and exits, are hardware systems. People networks are something else.

The seminal theoretical work about large-scale people networks comes from anthropology. In 1970, University of Minnesota anthropologists Luther P. Gerlach and Virginia H. Hine published *People, Power, Change; Movements of Social Transformation*, the first deep study of the large-scale structure of networks, based on their field work with two subcultures, the Pentecostal Movement and the Black Power Movement. Although the core ideologies of the two movements differed dramatically, Gerlach and Hine found that their structures were very similar and could be described as "a network—decentralized, segmentary, and reticulate."

"In the minds of many," they wrote, "the only possible alternative to a bureaucracy or a leader-centered organization is no organization at all." Rather, what they observed was a multi-leadered netting of sovereign participants threaded by common ideology.

Virginia Hine, who died in 1982, offered a concise summary of this work and gave it an historical perspective in her classic essay, "The basic paradigm of a future socio-cultural system." Hine introduced the concept of the SPIN, an acronym that stands for a "Segmented, Polycephalous, Ideological, Network" and suggested it as an "adaptive pattern of social organization for the global society of the future."

Contrasting a network with a bureaucracy that collapses like a table when one leg is cut off, Hine wrote, "A SPIN, on the other hand, is composed of autonomous *segments* that are organizationally self-sufficient, any of which could survive the elimination of all the others." A segment stands alone, and it stands with other segments.

The word *polycephalous* literally means "many heads." In traditional anthropology, Gerlach and Hine observed, a tribe without a single key leader is called "acephalous." In networks, Gerlach and Hine observed many leaders, with different people assuming leadership for different tasks. Not one key person but

5

many. Not one supreme authority, but rather many pools of responsibility.

"Frequently a leader is no more than *primus inter pares*, or first among equals, who speaks for the group only on certain occasions and can influence decision making rather than make decisions for the group," Hine wrote.

It is really the "I" of the SPIN that gives it its oomph. "The S, the P and the N represent organizational factors which can be handled at the sociological level of analysis," Hine wrote. "But the power of the unifying idea adds a qualitatively different element to the equation. The power lies in a deep commitment to a very few basic tenets shared by all."

A social network is a form of human organization. Evolutionary longevity testifies to the adaptability and indispensability of personal networking, probably as old as our species. Today, informal networking permeates our daily lives and operates at every level of even the most structured modern institutions. Our personal lives are sustained and complicated by clusters of connections that we call upon and that call upon us.

As though to bridge the distant past and the envisioned future, today we witness the emergence of a new form of network—group networks. Group networks are large-scale human organizations, like the previous social inventions of hierarchies and bureaucracies. A group that calls itself a network links individuals or groups or both. Often, groups within networks are organized along traditional hierarchic-bureaucratic lines yet maintain peer relationships at the network level.

In our sample of networks, we find two common patterns: (1) networks are whole systems composed of relatively autonomous participants; and (2) networks are created and sustained by bonds of shared values among participants.

Networks arise and function among equals. While nothing is absolutely self-reliant or totally independent, networks come alive through the relative autonomy of their participants, whether people, groups or large institutions. In networks, a respect for each entity, whether person, group or ecosystem, establishes the foundation for peer relationships.

Networks *decentralize decision making* through guidance by *many leaders* with *multiple layers* of intertwining connections and concerns in which people communicate as *nodes and links* that fade from view through *fuzzy boundaries*.

Networks are *decentralized* organizations. When a network disintegrates, its members stand free. Unlike the components of a centralized bureaucracy, the parts of a network are essentially independent and generalized. In networks, decision making is distributed; networks are coordinated, not controlled.

Networks are *polycephalous*, which literally means "many heads". Decentralized coordination requires distributed and fluid leadership. A network is always in a dynamic equilibrium between a few agreements on shared values and many disagreements on how to get from here to there. The *multiplicity* of leaders and viewpoints protects the network from domination by any one leader or any one opinion. This babble of equivalent voices is also what makes a network vulnerable to the impotence of factionalism.

Network participants connect horizontally, automatically generating two levels of activity at once, the level of each participant and the level of their network, their whole. As a network grows, local groups proliferate and new connections are made between networks, generating *multiple levels* of networking activity. All complex organizations, human or otherwise, develop a level structure. What distinguishes the network is that while generating levels, it also preserves autonomy and prerogatives for decision making in each participant at each level. In networks, information and decisions flow in all directions, up and down and across the layers of organization.

People in networks communicate as *nodes and links*, terms from communications theory that describe how physical networks, like the telephone, function. As a source or recipient of information, a person is a node. As an information carrier, making a connection between nodes, a person is a link. The essence of networking lies in the person-to-person relationship; it is people who write letters, memos, and business plans, talk in groups, place telephone calls, propose ideas, compile resources and cut deals. It is people who have and who transmit values.

Decentralized, polycephalous, multilayered, node/link networks have *fuzzy boundaries*. Connections based on shared values are bound to wax and wane as circumstances change for individuals and society. Just as we cannot completely enumerate everyone in our personal network, which in any case would change by tomorrow, so a group network rarely knows the extent of its membership, influence and resources.

An invisible, unweighable, intangible glue holds a network together. That glue is shared *values*. Values are the magnets that draw people into networks and hold them together. Values are binding forces. Values are the organizing principles that hold Peters' and Waterman's "excellent" corporations together. People in a network hold values shared by others in their network, even though values, above all, cannot be "held" in the physical sense of the word. Values are the principles that we live by, the perspective on life that our parents, and all the other institutions in our lives, pass along to us, and that we pass along to our children.

Making connections

To illustrate networking at work, we recount the beginning of our networking research and trace one of the journeys we explored in doing the research for this book: specifically, the pathway that led us to the experiential education network.

Our itinerary illustrates how networks function by forming links along lines of tenuous and tangential connections and related interests. Our odyssey is also a multileveled tale in the spirit of the late Yale psychologist Stanley Milgram, who found that anyone in the United States can reach anyone else by going through a statistical average of no more than 5.5 other people. In this example, we reached the universe of experiential education at our fourth "stop" of inquiry. Along the path of this particular itinerary, we passed by thousands of other groups and individuals.

Our tour began at Stop 0, in Newton, Massachusetts, where we sent our very first letter of inquiry to Robert A. Smith, III, at Stop 1, then living in Huntsville, Alabama.

Robert A. Smith, III, a retired US National Aeronautics and Space Adminstration (NASA) organizational management official, from Pine Apple, Alabama, is a networking pioneer, a quiet, backstage letter writer who connects people of like interests and ideas.

We first met Smith on the telephone in the mid-1970s, when he called at the suggestion of someone else, and a lifelong friendship was born. Bob Smith's personal story is exemplary of how one person without credentials, extensive education, or contacts "in high places" can nurture and create a one-person network that reaches around the globe.

The oldest of four children born in rural southern Alabama, Smith had what he calls an "eiditic capacity." He recalls, "We did not have kindergarten, and since we lived so far from town, my mother encouraged my imagination. From the time I was very young, I could entertain myself."

This self-motivating principle served him well later when, at the age of 43, in 1964, he suffered a nearly fatal heart attack that completely reshaped his life.

To recuperate, he sat for many hours in his backyard garden, where one day he had what he later understood to be a peak experience. "Suddenly, I became aware of how small I was in one sense, and how large I was in another," he explains. "I could feel my connection to the whole cosmos, and from there I was bolted into writing a dialogue between [authors] Henry Miller and Henry David Thoreau. I felt that I was at Walden Pond. I could actually see the cabin."

In one extraordinary moment, Smith burst open, like a spring pod in his lush garden, and began to experiment. In the summer of 1966, he spent two intense weeks at the National Training Laboratories in Bethel, Maine. "I began to read more. I studied Teilhard de Chardin, Goethe, and Jefferson, and developed the courage to dialogue with other people interested in the same ideas. And my wife, Dot, was very supportive of my emerging role change."

Smith's new path was unfolding at the same time that the US government, where he was now working as head of a NASA management research program, began to use WATS (Wide Area Telephone Service) lines, the first inexpensive long-distance phone service.

"I am a strong believer in synchronicity," Smith explains, "but people need to be connected to one another in order to form synergetic partnerships. So I started to use my WATS line to connect people."

By the end of the 1960s, Smith was on a "first name basis" with people who were completely outside his early life and experiences, nurturing a kind of human horticulture, companion planting people with similar interests in each other's mental garden. "I started directing people with similar ideas to one another," he says. "Then people began to 'use' me, and by that I mean 'use' in a very loving way, to find others with similar interests."

As the farewell gesture to his dear WATS at his retirement from NASA in 1977, Smith distributed his own catalog of contacts called "Try It! The Invisible College Directory and Network of Robert A. Smith, III." This concoction, organized by Smith's own feel for what is "good in the world," made public his personal network.

The Invisible College, photocopied and stapled together, was a cut-and-paste networking scrapbook of names, addresses, letter-heads, drawings and quotes, complete with cutouts of book reviews, newspaper articles, photographs, brochures and thought-provoking headlines. It included such diverse novelties as a picture of Stevie Wonder, a birthday announcement for a 4-year-old in Pine Apple, Alabama, quotes from Dane Rudhyar and Sri Chinmoy, a recipe for peanut pie from Angie Stevens in Plains, Georgia, an ad for a meditation bench, a photograph of Sasquatch/Big Foot positioned next to a snapshot of *Whole Earth Catalog* publisher Stewart Brand. It was half-typed, half-written by hand and crossed out, and it concluded, on page 82, with these words penned in by Smith: "As Bob Dylan would probably put it, this directory is a concern with 'chaos, watermelons, collard greens, clocks, medi-tation, space travel, everything'. It may reveal how diversity does not necessarily lead to structured pluralism or fragmented separa-tism but rather a unity with a profound mosaic."

When we began our network research, we began with Bob Smith. He responded immediately with names and addresses of nine more people to contact. Two of those referrals pick up the path of the experiential education network, Peter and Trudy Johnson-Lenz at Stop 2, in Lake Oswego, Oregon, and Robert Theobald at Stop 2A, in Wickenburg, Arizona. Both referred us on to Leif Smith at Stop 3, at the Office for Open Network in Denver, Colorado, but in two very different ways: the Johnson-Lenzes wrote us a note suggesting three contacts, the first of which was Leif Smith; Theo-bald's referral came, in characteristic networking fashion, indirectly.

At the time that Theobald received our letter, both he and the Johnson-Lenzes were active users of the Electronic Information

Exchange System (EIES), a computer conferencing system (see Chapter 7) based in Newark, New Jersey. Theobald submitted a copy of our letter to TRANSFORM, a group of people participating in a conference by that name on EIES. Among the people reading the letter in TRANSFORM was Charlton Price at Stop 2B, in Tacoma, Washington, then editor of the EIES newsletter *Chimo*. Price published our letter to Theobald in the electronic newsletter available to everyone on the computer system (which we subsequently learned about when Price sent us a copy of the newsletter item in the mail). Another user of the computer conferencing system, David Voremberg, at Stop 2C, in Somerville, Massachusetts (about fifteen minutes from our home), saw the same message in the electronic newsletter, called us on the phone and, among other suggestions, mentioned that we should contact Smith in Denver.

So we wrote to Smith at Stop 3. He and his coworker, Patricia Wagner, responded first with a telephone call and then with a follow-up packet of materials that included two years' of their tabloid newspaper (no longer published) containing several hundred more references, which we then combed looking for people and groups that seemed relevant and/or intriguing. Among these names was that of Maria Snyder, who became Stop 4, at the Association for Experiential Education, located in Denver, which published the *Journal of Experiential Education*. In contacting Snyder, we reached an entry point into the experiential education metanetwork.

Snyder responded quickly and fully, providing us with yet another list of names, including that of the Council for the Advancement of Experiential Learning (CAEL), at Stop 5, in Columbia, Maryland. CAEL is both a node point for research in experiential education, and one of twelve participating links in the Coalition for Alternatives in Postsecondary Education (CAPE), at Stop 6, in Frankfort, Kentucky. CAPE's General Secretary, Robert Sexton, responded to our inquiry, incidentally telling us that our letter "arrived after having been shredded by some kind of postal machine". Apparently, the letter remained sufficiently legible for him to understand what we were looking for, because he sent a pile of documents explaining CAPE's work.

Sexton referred us on to each of CAPE's twelve members. Eventually, we received a response from the Learning Resources

11

Network (LERN) at Stop 7, whose headquarters in Manhattan, Kansas, serves as the exchange point for 247 participating groups in forty states and Canada. LERN's universe includes both course-offering groups and learning exchanges, which operate through telephone referrals and information banks. The Kansas office sponsors conferences and workshops, provides technical assistance, and publishes a directory of its member organizations, one of which is at Boston College in Newton, Massachusetts, where our search for information began.

Global networking

From person to planet, networking is a medium with a message.

Consider the message hierarchy carries about social order and behavior, whether it's used in a family, corporation, or country. Bureaucracy, too, carries its messages, underlining every meeting and memo.

The networking message is "interdependence with independence."

This idea—that the process of networking itself carries a message and philosophy of human interaction regardless of what the networking is about—was introduced to us as a question. From the back of the room at the World Future Society conference in Washington, DC, in 1982, a question came about whether the "value glue" of a network had to be "good" values. Did we think, the questioner asked, that networks which formed around "bad" values and interests might still generate subtle benefits because of the process of networking itself? We admitted we did think so.

Values hold a network together, but of course one person's "good" values are another's "bad" values. Without judging a network's goals, values and objectives—its "ends"—we feel that networking *per se* can be beneficial because the "means" are participatory.

Our strongest impression about the rising tide of networking is the diversity of subjects and the congruence of form. As we increasingly see the terms "network" and "networking" used in a social context of a people/organizational form, we marvel at the consistency of concept within the multiplicity of applications.

The clear visual images of physical networks, from very small (webs and nets) to very large (roadways and talkways), are probably responsible for the spontaneous use of the word to describe a spread-out, multicentered, value-based group of people. This could describe the structure of a high tech company, an environmental group, or an international terrorist ring.

There is a coherence to the evolution of networking that is related to very large-scale social change. This shift, often phrased as movement from the Industrial to the Information Age, brings a new pattern of human organization, described by the word "network."

Writing in the earlier part of this century, the German sociologist Max Weber saw bureaucracy as a natural response to industrialism. Hierarchy, a word with ecclesiastical roots, emerged from the agricultural revolution that began 12,000 years ago. As later ages and forms of organization include earlier ones—as bureacracy included hierarchy and industrialism incorporated agriculturalism—so networking includes authority and specialization.

What is *old* about networking is rooted in the human pre-history of person-to-person contact that formed cooperative groups and made possible tools and language. What is *new* about networking is its promise as a global form of organization with roots in individual participation. A form that recognizes independence while supporting interdependence.

Networking can lead to a global perspective based on personal experience. The networks we know lead naturally to an image of the world-as-a-whole richly networked.

In his *Global Brain* audiovisual presentations, British author Peter Russell projects a suddenly new, powerful image that is now part of all human inheritance—the outside-looking-in true photograph of Planet Earth, delicately framed in deepest black. A global symbol of unity and interdependence. Literally. An image of us all that we all can hold in the metaphorical palm of our hand.

So, holding the world in your hand, visualize it organized as a single hierarchy. Think of it controlled by a few bureaucracies. Imagine it as an interplay of many networks.

If you already have had visions of global networks, you probably have sensed that the process of networking, wherever you find it, at whatever scale, is itself a contribution to the solutions of the global *problematique*.

Discovering the invisible planet

This book is about networks and networking. Networks are the links that bind us together, making it possible for us to share work, aspirations and ideals. Networking is a process of making connections with other people. This book is specifically concerned with the networking that creates the universe we call the Invisible Planet.

The Invisible Planet is not a place but a state of mind. Touching every area of our lives, there is an Invisible Planet, rarely seen on television or read about in newspapers. It is a state of ideas and visions and practical enterprises that people move in and out of depending on their moods and needs, a domain that is very new, and at the same time, very old.

In this special universe, health is perceived as the natural state of the body, cooperation is regarded as an effective way to meet basic needs, nature's ecological orchestra is revered as one unified instrument, business is regarded as an effective way to get vital work done, inner development is valued as a correlate to social involvement, and the planet is understood to be an interconnected whole.

There is an Invisible Planet and it is pulsating and expanding and unfolding through networking, an organic communications process that threads across interests, through problems, and around solutions. Networks are the meeting grounds for the inhabitants of this invisible domain. These flexible, vibrant organizations often exist without boundaries, bylaws, or officers. Networks are the lines of communication, the alternative express highways that people use to get things done. In crisis and in opportunity, the word spreads quickly through these people-power lines.

The Invisible Planet and its networks are complements. The Invisible Planet represents the ideas and the values. Networks and networking are the structures and processes through which the ideas and values come alive.

Inspired by a vision of a peaceful yet dynamic planet, entirely new cultures are emerging in our lands. They are connected by casual, ever-changing links among hundreds of millions of people with shared needs, values and aspirations. As short-lived, self-camouflaging, adisciplinary cross-hatches of activity, networks are invisible, uncountable and unpollable. Networks can be highly

14

active one day, and totally defunct the next. Every time a network comes to life its form is a little different.

Networks are stages on which dissonance is not only tolerated but encouraged, yet agreement is a common goal. They are the experimental seedbeds in which people risk stretching their creativity. Networks are efficient and effective; feedback is as spontaneous as telephones, mailings and meetings permit. Networks are often personal and friendly, supportive and affirming, critical and energizing. Networks can be intimate and immediate—at times they serve as our extended families, bonding people together as strongly as bloodlines.

Networks are the connections that make us all one people on one small planet near one small star. They are our newest and probably our oldest social invention. They are our gift to our children, who are natural networkers on the day they are born.

There are spokespeople on the Invisible Planet, but there are few exalted leaders, presidents, or boards of directors. There are people who serve as models, but there are few figureheads whose lives are to be cloned. There are entry points and connections—nodes and links—but there are few hierarchical structures along which individuals can advance. The Invisible Planet exists everywhere, from the smallest villages to the largest metropolises, offering anyone who shares the vision the opportunity to participate.

There is nothing to conquer on the Invisible Planet: there are only problems to solve, using personal resourcefulness as the provider of solutions. There are goods that are produced to be used but not thoughtlessly consumed, and obsoletism refers to an antiquated value system that arrogantly calls for winners and losers. Even the language people use is different: from a litany of overused cliches, people are finding novel ways to express themselves in optimistic, hope-filled phrases that help to create the reality toward which people are striving.

For every problem that is tossed up before us in newspapers and on television, someone—if not ten, twenty, or hundreds of someones—somewhere in the world is working on a solution. While the cameras have been turned in another direction and reporters have been preoccupied with following the multiple trails of disaster and corruption, networkers everywhere are creating the Invisible Planet, which is hidden to some and highly visible to others.

15

While the 1970s have been characterized in the United States as the age of narcissism, a more careful reading of the times reveals quite a different picture. The 1970s, we can now see, were a time of hard work, experimentation, and bridge building. It was during the 1970s that networks came into their own, offering a strong counterpoint to the centralized bureaucracies that now dominate people's lives.

- Although a women's health network may appear to have nothing to do with saving the whales, the declarations, functions, and styles of both groups indicate that they are operating out of the same, mutualistic concerns for a world in which honor and protection are accorded to all living beings.
- While a group working for disarmament may appear to have nothing in common with an executive breakfast group, these two vital networks are both working to engage people in re-creating the world around them.
- Even though there is no formal connection between a Native American sovereignty network and a group of communicators in a major religious denomination, they share some deep conceptual connections and a value system that honours individual choice and cultural pluralism.
- Whereas an organization development network may think it has nothing in common with a hospice, on closer examination it is apparent that both cherish values that support people's control over their own lives.

These connections cross categories, transcending individual issues. It is a shared value system that defines the pattern of a "metanetwork," a network of networks, an immense subculture.

Our Invisible Planet exists as a pattern of connections and values, a complex latticework of hope and despair, anger and love, fantasy and reality, descriptions of problems, and examples of solutions. While some might say that optimism is unrealistic at this point in history, networkers counter with the belief that the future we create together is a matter of attitude and that while the doomsayers are important beacons, they spotlight only a portion of reality. Every day, every new situation, every new problem is a challenge and a potential for beneficial change.

The Invisible Planet is entered by taking another look at what is going on around us and recognizing the connections and nascent links among all the little islands of hope. If the idea of the Invisible Planet seems remote, if not a fantasy, here in Chapter 1, reconsider this feeling after wandering through the examples in this book. Look closely at the networks working in areas you know something about and imagine the simple links that would carry you into the nearest conceptual neighborhoods of this planet of the mind.

One very special network: the Boston Women's Health Book Collective

The Canadian government is the only one in the world with a "health promotion" directorate in its cabinet. Each year, the Health Promotion Directorate's provincial directors meet for a few days for inspiration and renewal.

Norma Swenson was among those who spoke at the Fall 1984 seminar in Montreal. A coauthor of *Our Bodies, Ourselves*, the book that changed the course of women's health around the world, Norma sparkles when she speaks with words long on statistics. She is one member of a small but influential network—the Boston Women's Health Book Collective.

A few days later in Watertown, Massachusetts, Judy Norsigian, a Collective member and networker *extraordinaire*, is seated at her desk, flooded with light for her television interview. A television reporter, a woman in her thirties (not much older than Judy), is questioning the women's health activist about the bill before the Massachusetts State Legislature that would license out-of-hospital birth centers. Speaking carefully and articulately, with the casual ease of someone who has done hundreds of interviews, Judy explains the excellent care record of free-standing birth centers.

Just a few feet away, Pamela Morgan, another member of the Collective, is writing a letter that will be sent to scores of women who are participating in the production of *The New Our Bodies, Ourselves* (published in 1985).

Less than a desk's distance from Pamela, Jane Pincus, another Collective member who moved back to Boston in 1980, after five years in northern New England, is on the telephone with a woman who is trained in *shiatsu*—the Japanese pressure point massage technique that releases blocks, aches and spasms in the body. Jane is inviting the masseuse to give a demonstration at the upcoming meeting of the Rising Sun Feminist Health Alliance, the network of northeast US women's health activists that meets semiannually as a support group and a retreat from the hectic, stressful pace that these women maintain.

Behind Jane, two more members of the Collective—Vilunya Diskin, who has just arrived from a day of classes at the Harvard School of Public Health, where she is studying for a PhD in population studies, and Norma, returned from Montreal—are absorbed in a planning meeting in the office's conference space, reviewing their ideas about children's nutrition in preparation for a meeting with two people from a large New York foundation.

Within a few moments, Judy's television interview is finished and she switches places with Jane. Now Jane is on camera, explaining the traps that women have been led into by pharmaceutical manufacturers who market products without sufficiently testing them. Judy, in the meantime, is answering a call from a woman in Lexington, Kentucky, who needs information about the harmful side effects of taking phenobarbital while on the Pill. As Judy cites the *New England Journal of Medicine* study that documents the potentially toxic effects of combining these two prescription drugs, the telephone rings again; she excuses herself, momentarily putting the first caller on hold while she answers the incoming call from an Ann Arbor woman who needs help in preparing public testimony on an out-of-hospital birth center bill before the Michigan legislature.

For the first ten years, the group had no office, operating out of the women's homes. By 1980, they rented an office furnished with donated chairs, couches, filing cabinets, shelves and desks. All available space is being used to good effect: hanging plants frame posters on women's rights; directories of women's action groups are heaped next to stacks of another of the Collective's books, *Ourselves and Our Children*; and literature racks are filled with articles, pamphlets and reports about menopause, cervical caps, Depo-Provera, DES, sterilization, breast cancer, hysterectomy, and numerous other topics. Cartons packed with copies of *Nuestros Cuerpos, Nuestras Vidas*, the Spanish-language edition of *Our Bodies, Ourselves*, which the Collective publishes and distributes itself, are draped with antique silk scarves, making an aesthetic virtue of the reality of limited space. Information—the raw material, the energy resource, and the finished product of networking—transforms a one-time classroom into a living, breathing, encyclopedia on women's health.

No sooner are television interviews, telephone calls and planning sessions complete than the foundation visitors arrive, two of scores of people who pass through the Collective's doors each month. In the past few weeks alone, people from Quebec, Senegal, Bangladesh, Ireland, Brazil and Japan have visited, reporting on their countries while gathering more data for use at home.

"We all have the same issues," Judy explains to the foundation people, stuffing envelopes while she talks. "Women abroad have the same concern about empowerment as we do, the same interest in gaining control over their lives, the same problems with violence against women. Even though they may manifest differently, the central issues are really the same. In India, brides are burned to death if their dowries are too small; here in the United States, violence takes the form of rape and battering."

What are the women's credentials for doing this work? the foundation people ask in a curious, rather than confronting, manner.

The women have created their own impeccable credentials. "That's precisely the point," explains Norma, who obtained a master's degree in public health at Harvard after participating in the initial rewrite of the original edition of *Our Bodies, Ourselves*, first issued under the title *Women and Their Bodies* in 1970. "We're not medical people; we're simply a group of women who wanted to understand more about ourselves."

The telephone rings again as the foundation people try to understand how a group of "uncredentialed" women could have written a best-selling book with sales exceeding two million copies and translations into more than a dozen languages, then gone on to write another popular book, *Ourselves and Our Children*, while fulfilling speaking engagements, which average about one per week, participating in numerous projects and special-interest groups, and managing to maintain long-term marriages, weather family traumas, and raise more than a dozen children among themselves.

Norma answers the phone, and agrees to do a ten-minute interview with a feminist from Holland, who arrives at the office twenty minutes later to take pictures of the Collective in action.

Why a women's health movement?

Why would a group of women feel the need to write a book about women's health? Why would the response from other women be so overwhelming? The Boston Women's Health Book Collective serves as an unparalleled entry point into the international women's health network.

Western medicine has strayed from its ancient lineage in the healing arts, a gigantic resource of timeworn natural remedies from many traditions, passed along from shaman to shaman, from midwife to midwife, from healer to healer. Whereas once healing was revered as a gift, today medicine is a prestigious profession whose perks increase as doctors advance higher on the medical ladder. Although understanding the "person as a whole" was once an unquestioned assumption of healers, today subspecialists have cropped up to minister to every minute subdivision of the body.

We can see this principle in action by following a woman who would see a succession of doctors if she chose the prevailing North American medical approach to childbearing. An obstetrician is no longer really a pregnancy specialist; s/he is the "general prac- titioner" of parturition, making referrals to an endocrinologist, a radiologist for the "older" woman, a neurologist, an orthopedist, and finally a neonatologist, the successor to the pediatrician, for once the baby emerges from the womb, the obstetrician is officially off the case.

In order to even understand her course of treatment for the "disease of giving birth," a pregnant woman has to become conversant with a whole new language of medical "technese." As the traditional testing ground for medications and anesthesias to be used in other forms of surgery, obstetrics is not a fixed science. Routines and methods come in and go out of fashion; today's universal use of epidural anesthesia is just as quickly replaced by tomorrow's new order to screen every pregnant woman over 35 by amniocentesis.

However, to regard these impermanent routines as fads fails to recognize the true seriousness and long-term harmfulness of using pregnant women as guinea pigs. Recall the thalidomide tragedy, in which an untested drug was prescribed for pregnant women as a sedative in the early 1960s, causing severely disfiguring birth defects in their children, or the diethylstilbestrol (DES) catastrophe of the 1950s, 1960s and early 1970s, in which millions of babies were exposed to this dangerous hormone before birth, resulting in an unusually high rate of a rare form of vaginal cancer in the girls and testicular abnormalities and sterility in the boys.

The natural stages of women's physical maturation have been medicalized, objectified as an illness that must be treated—beginning with menarche, continuing through pregnancy and childbirth, and ending with menopause. Painkillers and mood elevators are routinely prescribed for menstruation; caesarean delivery—birth by surgery—is fast becoming the preferred treatment of many obstetricians, with the number of surgical births having quadrupled from 1968 to 1981; and hormones, tranquilizers and routine hysterectomies have become the standardized treatment for women in menopause.

The tampon fiasco, which received so much publicity, is only the tip of the medical-malfeasance iceberg in regard to women's health.

- Intrauterine devices (IUDs), widely prescribed in the late 1960s and early 1970s and currently being marketed in Third World countries, have been found to induce many harmful side effects, from intense pain and excessive bleeding to permanent uterine damage and infertility.
- In Puerto Rico, more than one-third of the women of childbearing age have been sterilized. According to the Committee to End Sterilization Abuse in New York, most of the women consented to the operation without knowing that surgical sterilization is rarely, if ever, reversible.
- Hysterectomies have become the second most frequently performed operation in the United States, with 25 percent of all women over 50 having had one, in spite of the fact that the operation is major surgery and has been estimated to be unnecessary in as many as 30 to 50 percent of all cases. The fastest rise has been for younger women. In 1980, half of the 649,000 hysterectomies were done on women under 45. Of all adult women in the US today, 62 percent will have had a hysterectomy or oophorectomy (ovary removal) by the time they are 70.
- More that 20 percent of all births in the United States are caesarean deliveries, accompanied by an alarmingly high postoperative infection rate of about 25 percent. While the overall

maternal death rate in childbirth has dropped since the turn of the century due to public health advances, the maternal death rate from caesareans remains much higher than that of vaginal deliveries.

● The modified radical mastectomy remains the treatment of choice of many surgeons for breast cancer, despite the fact that other less traumatic and less mutilating methods have been found to produce equal or better survival rates.

Over the past twenty years, many women have begun to recognize this unhealthful pattern and have responded in many ways: they have developed their own networks, through which they can meet their own health needs; they have critiqued the existing system of care and worked to change it; and they have created the field of "women's health for women," with its own research, books, conferences and, ultimately, philosophy. Where the medical community, in which 90 percent of the doctors are men, has regarded women's bodies as "other" and their physical maturation as disease, the women's health movement has advanced a model of women as "ourselves," as healthy people whose life changes are moments of opportunity and awakening.

Making history

The history of the Collective offers a valuable insight into how networks form, jell and persist over time without elaborate planning, self-conscious statements of purpose, or long-term goals. The Boston Women's Health Book Collective, one of the oldest and most successful of the networks we have learned about, just happened.

"We never set out to *do* anything," Vilunya recalls. "You don't plan to bring a group of twelve women together, enlist the help of hundreds of others, write a book that sells 250,000 copies over two years through 'underground' distribution with a price that is lowered from $.75 to $.30, face the choice of which major publisher to sign with, and then find your book on the *New York Times* best-seller list for three years."

"Everything flowed organically from one thing to another," she says. "And it's still growing."

Indeed, eleven of the twelve original members of the group (the twelfth moved to Canada in the early 1970s and one remains active from her home in California) are still actively involved and two new members have been added, representing a cross-section of middle and upper-middle-class, college-educated white women ranging in age from their late thirties to late fifties.

"We've seen one another through four new babies (making twenty-one children in all), four divorces and three weddings, one case of the hot flashes, some dramatic long affairs, three children going off to college and nine are in the midst of adolescence," writes Collective member Wendy Coppedge Sanford in *Heresies* magazine.

The Collective got its start in May 1969, when Nancy Hawley, an antiwar activist involved in one of the first informal women's liberation groups in Boston, gave a workshop on "Women and Their Bodies" at a women's conference.

"We decided to have the conference because our weekly women's meetings at Massachusetts Institute of Technology (MIT), where several of our husbands studied or worked, were too limiting. Every week, more and more women showed up, all by word-of-mouth," Nancy remembers.

"It was a very exciting time," Jane reflects. "The air was full of rhetoric—even karate was in the air."

Nancy's workshop was the catalytic event that set everything else in motion: the sign-up sheet at the workshop became the mailing list for a group that gathered over the summer with the task of making a list of "good" obstetricians and gynecologists. Calling themselves "The Doctor's Group," they consisted of ten women, five of whom are still in the Collective: Jane, Nancy and Vilunya (all friends previously), and Esther Rome and Paula Doress, both of whom had attended the conference where Nancy gave her workshop.

By the fall, the "good" doctors list was abandoned, and the women had begun to research topics of interest to them, unconsciously creating the chapters that would ultimately appear in *Our Bodies, Ourselves*. "I was very interested in the postpartum experience," Esther says, "because my mother had had a very serious depression after I was born. So I went to the library and found that practically nothing had been written about it. All of us were having the same experience in the libraries: there was no information to be found. That was when we started to put forward our own experiences and our own knowledge. We never set out to 'discover' anything—we only wanted to learn more to evaluate what the doctors were saying."

The topics of interest created so much new information—and so much excitement—that the women decided to offer the material in the form of a course for other women.

"I was in a very serious postpartum depression when I went to the first meeting, and I vividly remember every moment of that night," Wendy says fifteen years later. Esther prodded her to attend the course; they knew each other because their husbands were in architecture school together. "We broke up into small groups, and a woman started talking about postpartum depression. It was an extraordinary moment of release for me when I realized that I was not to blame for my depression. I took that energy and poured it back into the group for the next ten years."

The MIT course was also the Collective entry point for three others: Pamela Berger, Joan Ditzion and Ruth Bell, who maintains her ties to the Boston group even though she now lives in Los Angeles. (Ruth is also the major author of *Changing Bodies, Changing Lives*, modeled after *Our Bodies, Ourselves*, and geared for teens.) Out of this core working group of nine (and literally scores of other women who dropped in and out over the next year or so), the "topics" were expanded to fill a book called *Women and Their Bodies*, including chapters on anatomy and physiology, socialization, venereal disease, pregnancy, abortion, postpartum depression, sexuality, birth control, and political analysis of medical institutions.

For the first time in history, a group of women had written a book about themselves, for themselves, a fact that was later translated into the subtitle of their book ("By and for Women"). *Women and Their Bodies*, run off on newsprint by a local "movement" printer (the New England Free Press), and stapled together, was an overnight success. By the time of the second printing, the women had unequivocally claimed their work as their own by retitling their book *Our Bodies, Ourselves*.

"Every day orders flooded the office of the Free Press," Judy (who joined the group with Norma, as the last two members, in the fall of 1971) told *New Roots* magazine (no longer published). "Women in the Boston area sent it to their friends all over the US, who sent it to their friends, and within two years, 250,000 were sold without spending a cent on advertising." In addition to the friendship network, thousands of books were sold through the burgeoning women's movement on US college campuses.

It seemed that everyone was talking about this $.30 book, including New York publishers who contacted the group with attractive offers to republish it—offers that threw the group into six months of soul searching. While they knew that mass distribution would reach even more women, they were very wary of corporate profit. Setting out clear and unusual demands to the publisher—including final control over the cover and all promotional advertising as well as unlimited discount copies for distribution at nonprofit women's clinics—the group was pleased to find Simon & Schuster agreeing to its terms. In order to sign the contract, the group had to be an "entity." They formed a nonprofit corporation and called themselves the "Boston Women's Health Book Collective."

"We never had a solemn moment when we said, 'We are us,'" Wendy remarks, demonstrating how a network may close off a part of itself naturally and become a formal organization. "We never needed to say to anyone, 'You can't join'," Jane adds. "We were simply making our book, and who we were was obvious."

The group has met weekly ever since—through three major revisions of the 1973 Simon & Schuster edition (issued in 1976), a Spanish-language version of the book, one update of the book in 1979, and the conception and creation of *Ourselves and Our Children*, published in 1978 by Random House (the original competitor with Simon & Schuster). In addition, the group has also published two basic pamphlets on subjects of current concern, *Sexually Transmitted Diseases and How to Avoid Them* and *Menstruation*, and has coauthored the *International Women and Health Resource Guide*. In 1985, *The New Our Bodies, Ourselves* was published by Simon & Schuster.

It is astonishing to realize that this enormous web of connections began when one woman gave a workshop attended by thirty other women on a sunny day in May 1969, three weeks to the day after her second child was born. Yet this is precisely how networks coalesce: an individual makes a small gesture in a larger environment of people who are thinking along the same lines. The context allows the network to emerge naturally among the people involved. No one person is responsible; rather, everyone is.

CHAPTER 3

Networking in practice

As word of the power of networking spreads, so do its areas of application multiply. Networking is now being used intentionally in nearly every sphere of human activity.

In this chapter, we profile the deliberate use of networking within a mainstream Protestant denomination, a nonprofit organization that helps corporations to exchange information about the employment of disabled people, and a multinational consulting firm that describes its organizational structure as a network.

Connections 84

"Confer" is a word first used in 1538 that combines *con*, meaning *together*, and *ferre*, meaning *intensive*. "Coming together intensively" summarizes the essence of those events we call conferences. Many networks trace their beginnings to one "special" conference or meeting in their past, and many networks host conferences as a major organizational function.

Networks are born and grow through alternating phases of face-to-face interaction and cooperation-at-a-distance. Conferences and other types of meetings provide periodic opportunities to reaffirm or redefine shared values, to establish and realign relationships, to conduct work, and to have fun with others.

Besides whatever is communicated at a conference through its *content*, there are also the messages generated through the conference *structure*. Conferences usually have a title, often a theme, and frequently a specific purpose. Conferences also have an organizational structure and may be interpreted using hierarchical, bureaucratic and networking models.

Conferences are media of organizational expression. While a

conference design inevitably makes some *metacomment* about authority and values within the sponsoring group, it may also be a conscious experiment in social organization. As intense, brief social forms, conferences sometimes become microcosms of their particular universes and new organizational configurations are tried.

A network is a whole of free-standing participants cohering through shared values, goals, and/or interests. A conference design can easily experiment with variations on this definition, creating enduring social wholes from dynamic, independent human parts—people and groups. Creating opportunities for peers to come together, for new leaders to emerge, for old groups to congregate, and for new groups to form are among the reasons for using a network conference design.

Somewhere along the spectrum from very centralized to very decentralized meetings, the clear distinction between form and content begins to fade. Where a traditional meeting schedule is built from blocks of well-specified time, a network schedule perceives the time *between* the content blocks as equally important. As many a wag has noted, the best (most fun, meaningful, profitable) time at a conference is had at lunch, in the pool, at the bar, or wherever, with other participants.

Our interest in network conference design took a big leap one hot August day in 1983 when the telephone rang. Robert Wood, a New York management consultant, was calling on behalf of a large organization in need of networking skills. The context for the need, Wood explained, was a conference planned for May 1984, which would bring together the networks among the organization's 3.2 million members, a gathering of those in agreement and those in conflict.

We were intrigued. Wood was calling for the Presbyterian Church (USA), which had its unique slant on a common networking problem. After a hundred years of Civil War-induced separation into two churches—a national northern church and a regional southern church—and several previous attempts at reunification, the two churches merged in June 1983.

The merger involves two central offices, one in Atlanta, Georgia, and one in New York City, twenty synods comprising 195 presbyteries (literally "ecclesiastical court in presbyterian Church composed of all the ministers and a ruling elder from each parish in its district") that arise from 11,662 churches attended by the three million people.

The mandate of the reunited church? *Inclusiveness*, an idea that was easier to talk about than to actualize in a church which now included dozens of networks of difference—in ideology, theology and constituency. It sounded to us like a model of the world.

By the time we entered the process, planning for the May 1984 conference had been underway for more than a year, under the guidance of Sandra Grear, Director of the Communications Unit of the Presbyterian Church (USA).

Grear, a radio and television broadcaster, took her position in the church's New York office with the dream of creating the conference.

"We wanted to bring together a microcosm of the church and put into practice what we say we are about. The church is being restructured, which gives us the opportunity to reorganize. We don't have the luxury of pointing a finger at the hierarchy any more and saying, 'How are you going to make this work?' *We* have to make this work", she explains.

Thus, Grear and her colleagues embarked on a two-year planning process that involved dozens of people at all levels of the church hierarchy who considered everything from conference site and dates to attendees to menus to content areas.

The result was a five-day invitational conference, attended by 200 "connectors" and "communicators" in the church, who congregated in a Kansas City hotel. "Connectors" came primarily from special-interest areas within the greater church, while "communicators" were those who work in media, both inside and outside this major Protestant denomination.

The "content areas" already had been decided when we entered the process: cross-cultural communication, the Myers-Briggs Type Indicator (a psychological profile based on Jung's classic "archetypes"), networks and networking, and theological perspectives.

Each content area had its own team of presenters. The keynote speaker was *Megatrends* author John Naisbitt.

When the conference was over, Grear received the master link in a motorcycle drive chain that had been distributed in three-link pieces to each of the content area presenters as key chains. "The master link is invisible in the chain," explained William Moore, pastor of the Sharon (Pennsylvania) Community Presbyterian

Church who served on the three-member conference "tracking team" with Grear and Wood.

Lunch, dinner, and morning and afternoon break times were all scheduled as integral parts of the conference. Two worship services also took place, the first on the opening night of the conference, and the second on the last day, Sunday morning.

Throughout the conference, reference was made to two possible images of the reunited church, with its differing concerns: the traditional melting pot, where immigrants from the various regions dissolve indistinguishably, and the salad bowl, where each ingredient maintains its integrity. The preference at the conference seemed to be for the salad.

Just before the conference began, Robert F. Cramer, who publishes *RFC News*, a newsletter about communication in the ecumenical community, and *Church News International*, a daily online press service *a la* UPI on NewsNet, put out his newsletter with these cautionary words about Connections 84:

> The first large-scale experiment in group process, extended to an entire church denomination, is about to begin. . . . It's daring, and forward looking, and it should creatively set the stage for many years of participatory power sharing in one of America's major churches. But it's bound to unleash a lot of frustration and hostility and it could backfire. It's a risky idea.

No one knew what would happen at a conference that included pro-life and pro-choice activists, evangelicals and gay/lesbian ordination advocates, "racial/ethnics" and "tall steeple ministers" (to speak Presbyterianese).

And no one knew what would happen with a conference design that left open the possibility of on-site changes in order to respond to the evolution of the conference itself.

It worked. Cramer's postconference issue (he attended as a "communicator" and took extensive notes on his lap-top computer) expresses the enthusiasm of the participants, and captures the more subtle meaning of the event as history.

> In a nutshell, what happened was that people's notions of communication shifted perceptibly towards the larger notion of interpersonal connections.

People began to think less about media products and more about interpersonal processes.

During a two-year [planning] process an elemental theory of communication was explored and was returned to time after time: compelling communication occurs in what are now being called networks, that is, the circle(s) of one's associates.

Alongside that was the realization that there are many networks in place in the church which function very well—Presbyterians for Pro-Life (represented at Connections 84) is a good example.

And, planners had a growing awareness that networks of networks can provide vehicles, fuel, and steering mechanisms for very large, diverse populations—maybe even for a 3.2-million member denomination.

The strength of the conference was that it was conceptual, not technical. The media experts formed a network to share their concerns—but they were only one of many networks formed at the conference which will continue. It was a visible and explicit picturing of the future—media concerns taking their place as only one of many aspects of human intercommunication. In this sense, the conference was, as it tried to be, a microcosm of the entire denomination in the present as well as in the future.

Two years later, Connections 84 continues, with regional "Connections" conferences having been held in several locations, a periodic newsletter, regular telephone conference calls, and an online computer conferencing system called PresbyNet.

"Our behaviour must model our beliefs," Grear says. "Networking must extend to all forms of media, and not be exclusive of any. No one is to be left out. This is a global community."

Networking abilities for jobs

At the Massachusetts Division of Employment Security, housed in one of the newer buildings in Boston's Government Center, the staff jokes that if job applicants can find Katharine Rolfe's office, they ought to get the job. Down narrow corridors, past unnamed offices, and within a small cubicle with a large picture of Gloria Steinem on the crowded bulletin board, sits Kathy Rolfe.

Kathy Rolfe is a networker. When we arrived at her office on a rainy day in August 1985, she looked straight at Jeff and said, "I know you". Indeed she did. They went to both high school and college together. From the University of New Hampshire, Rolfe moved to Boston, began her career in state government, and soon became active in disability issues.

On the day we saw her, Rolfe was wearing "polycephalous" (see Chapter 9) hats, both as chair of the Governor's Commission on the Employment of the Handicapped and as the sparkplug behind the Massachusetts Corporate Partnership Program (MCPP).

We couldn't meet in Rolfe's cubicle; we were too many. Besides the two of us and Kathy, there were two others: Cecily Lewis, Program Coordinator and first staff employee for MCPP, and Edward M. Kennedy, Jr, who was the reason the interview had come about in the first place.

In Massachusetts, Kennedy watching is a political spectator sport. Every election, the media is filled with reports about which Kennedy (the third generation has come of age) is running (or not) for which office.

So it was one Sunday morning that a *Boston Globe* headline caught our attention: "Ted Kennedy Jr says he won't run for Congress."

The second sentence leapt out of the page: "Kennedy said . . . that he was eager to pursue his role in a networking organization to get jobs for the handicapped."

The article went on: "Kennedy spoke enthusiastically about what he called a networking role for the foundation where he gets successful employers of the handicapped to get new companies to listen to them."

A little networking goes a long way. Though the name, purpose, origins, activities, and Kennedy's role in the organization all were incorrect in the article, there was just enough information there to enable us to find Cecily Lewis, who spent the first five minutes of our initial telephone conversation clearing up the facts. People looking for jobs and money had been calling all morning.

As Lewis told MCPP's story, it sounded more and more like a networking organization. We requested an interview.

The Massachusetts Corporate Partnership Program states its goal

32

on its simple, one-color brochure: "to increase the number of employers participating in activities which promote opportunities for handicapped persons."

In essence, MCPP is developing a comprehensive database of resources for employment of disabled people. Specifically, what MCPP does is to link those who need information about employing disabled people with those who have already gone through that process. MCPP *is*, as Kennedy says, a networking organization.

An example from Lewis: "Say a company wants to hire a blind person but doesn't know what kind of accommodations to make. We can search our database and give them the names of other companies that have done that. Many companies think they'll have to spend thousands and thousands of dollars to hire a blind person. But that's not true. Lots can be done with very little money."

Beginning with what Rolfe describes as a "very low key approach," and lacking what she calls "the desire to build an empire," MCPP gathers information.

Kennedy, 23, has been hired as Marketing Coordinator to help sell the idea to corporations.

Corporations participate in the program as "corporate partners," which they cannot become until they have done "the activities." "Activities" include:

- expanding job possibilities—"Take a fresh look at all job descriptions [and their] requirements. Do they inadvertently screen out disabled people?"
- expanding education and training of disabled people—"Provide subcontract work to local rehabilitation organizations whenever possible."
- public relations—"Make yourself and your company executives available to speak about employment of disabled persons at local service clubs."
- inhouse motivation—"The CEO should declare his/her own personal commitment to the employment of disabled people."
- expanding employee awareness of disabled people—"Include articles about successfully employed disabled workers in inhouse magazines, and newsletters."

Once the activities are behind them, corporations are *bona fide* partners, and thus able to answer questions for other companies.

33

Each corporate partner fills out an extensive questionnaire, which doubles as an educational tool.

"We never do mass mailings of questionnaires," Rolfe says. "We ask people these questions and the questions cause the employers to think of things they've never considered before."

Rolfe describes MCPP's "diffusion of innovation" theory as the "old New Hampshire snowball dance. You start with one couple, then they split and get another partner, and so on."

Corporate partners recruit new corporate partners. But Rolfe is not fixated on numbers of corporations involved; she envisions what she calls "the soup to nuts approach."

"We're looking for five or six companies to volunteer to do everything," she says, citing possible involvement of every echelon of the corporation from the CEO down to the shop floor level.

Along the way, MCPP is creating information resources that have never existed before. Besides the Corporate Partner database which includes information on some 250 companies, MCPP has assembled the first comprehensive statewide directory of social service agencies involved with rehabilitation.

"Each of the particular agencies had its own directory of affiliated organizations, but there was no single source that included things like Joe's Rehab workshop in Pittsfield," Lewis said.

Referring to her Kennedy coworker, Rolfe says, "He wasn't hired for his name. He was hired for his public relations skills. We needed someone who could market the program with the credibility of being disabled."

Rolfe first met Kennedy at the 1985 Boston Marathon, where he fired the starting shot for the wheelchair competition. They arranged to meet a few weeks later in Washington at a meeting of the President's Committee on Employment of the Handicapped where Kennedy gave a presentation on how new technologies can be applied to disability issues.

One year out of college, and extremely active in the public sector on disability issues, Kennedy was ready to apply what he knew to what he considers the key issue.

"Jobs. It's all about jobs. If people can work, then they can be independent," he says leaning forward as if to put even more drive behind his words.

Kennedy has been "disabled" since he was 12 when his right leg was amputated as a result of bone cancer. His ceremonial duties at the Boston Marathon are typical of his engagement with disability issues.

Tall and in excellent physical condition, he's a good advertisement for "abilities rather than disabilities," as he says. "If you call up for a job and say, 'I'm in a wheelchair, and I can't go up a flight of stairs', instead of saying, 'I'm a computer programmer and I know six languages', you don't get anywhere."

"It's all got to come from the grassroots," he says, dismissing the idea that working at the powerbroker level has much to do with disability issues.

In that regard, Rolfe says, "We're administered by the Information Center for Individuals with Disabilities, a private nonprofit." Thus they're plugged in to one of the key nerve centers for disability issues in the state.

Rolfe's hope is for MCPP to be a model for others. "As far as we know there's nothing else like this," she says.

Her program for success is very straightforward. She cites her three basic rules: "(1) KISS—Keep it simple, stupid; (2) If it's not fun, don't do it; and (3) No mass mailings—make it person-to-person like the old New Hampshire snowball dance."

Networking Arthur D. Little-style

Robert Kirk Mueller (pronounced Miller) is a student of networking. A chemical engineer and a member over the past several decades of some thirty boards of directors, he is Chairman of the Board of Arthur D. Little, Inc. (ADL), an international research and consulting firm.

Our correspondence with Bob Mueller began some years back, prompted by a 1980 letter from our old friend Robert A. Smith, III. Smith enclosed an exciting article by Mueller titled "Leading-edge leadership." In it, Mueller called for "more leaders and fewer executives," and pointed to "the recent trend toward plural management organizational structures." He maintains that "a free-form organizational style is probably the most likely to survive" and that "peer systems of management with a minimum of hierarchical structure are more likely to retain the leading-edge leader."

Much to our delight, Bob Mueller was one of the first people to join The Networking Institute. We then met Bob face-to-face in July 1984, when he called together a group of ADL people who were concerned with the concepts of networking either directly or peripherally in their work.

A year later we met again, this time in Bob's office at Acorn Park, ADL's main research facility, in Cambridge, Massachusetts. It is a rather simple place for the chairman of the board of a multinational corporation. Painted white cinder block walls, large glass windows in the best public school tradition, plain industrial carpet on the floors. The art is intriguing, mostly folk pieces from the Third World. One wall holds a plaque board, with seals of the countries in which Bob has worked in various activities.

"If you were from Argentina," he explained as we were leaving, "I'd have put the Argentine plaque in the middle."

Thoughtfully, he had put the first issue of the *Networking Journal*, which we had recently published, on the coffee table.

We originally knew Bob as an astute observer and theorist of management and large-scale organization, by way of his 1974 article, "Wider horizons for the corporate board."

A decade later, the news release on his speech to the Society of Professional Management Consultants was bannered: SOCIAL AND PROFESSIONAL NETWORKING VITAL TO SURVIVAL OF INSTITUTIONS. In his address, Bob offers his view of the relevance of networking to large-scale organizations:

As a result of our structured institutional worlds being under siege, new strains of organization are forming in contemporary human activity. While this is a normal, evolutionary phenomenon, I suggest it presents an opportunity for us to think about empowering human networks in order to compensate for some of the inadequacies of a hierarchical-type organization.

Organization, as we know it, is obsolete in the information society in which we now exist. Those of us in management who weave human networks have confounded ourselves and our establishment's thinking. These human networks are thriving while our staid and rigid organizations heave and struggle to be effective or even to survive. Something fundamental is happening in our organized society . . . centered on the intuitive notion that, somehow or some way, networking may be basic to organizing and managing people in the future.

Bob Mueller believes in some theory and lots of practice. His ideas about networks and network management are rooted in his experience, particularly at ADL, which is the focus of this interview.

A society of professionals

Bob Mueller: "Arthur D. Little is a nonhierarchical, relatively egalitarian organization which is peer-driven. In one sense, it appears to be disorganized. On the other hand, it's a mobile, organic type of organization with minimal hierarchy. The only hierarchy comes when we get a task or engagement or assignment—a 'case,' which becomes a contract. When General Motors or somebody asks us to do a research job, we assign that to an individual who is qualified by a peer selection process and ratified by the contract office. That person is the prime contractor and she or he solicits staff from the rest of ADL around the world or outside and runs a project as project manager. In that sense, we have a hierarchy in that we have a case leader, an engagement leader, who is responsible for client relationships, for writing the proposal, for billing the client, certain administrative procedural tinfoil, if you will, to package it up in.

"The contracting office watches for conflicts of interests, and that sort of thing. But that hierarchical form has a short half-life in that it dies when the project's over. Then everybody goes out and works under other hierarchies. You may work part-time or full-time on an assignment. You may be working on three or four at the same time, just like a dentistwith three chairs.

"Our hierarchy is episodic. The organization is made up of what I call 'tribal groups'. Basically, tribal groups are disciplinary or industry groups where the economists are in one tribe or those who know the electronics industry are in another group. But they're always exporting their services out to other groups because most of our work is multidisciplinary. Tribal professionals get together because they can exchange information in their discipline. It's completely segmented, like a beehive.

"The way in which we get things done is by networking, by

going directly to somebody by reputation or by referral or from any place that you know to say, 'Who knows something about hospital management or boards of directors?' And, they'll say, 'Well, Dr Kasten knows something about that. Go to him.' Then Dr Kasten refers them to somebody else. So that's the way the staff is recruited.

"Because Arthur D. Little [the founder] was a chemical engineer, the theme of the chemical industry—chemical engineering, physics and related sciences—is quite profound in the organization. We're rooted in that. We do a lot of laboratory work, a lot of consulting, a lot of survey work, a lot of publications that are in the chemical industry.

"With ADL, we have what I call the 'chemical estate.' We have a 'chemical estate' network and its registry identifies 300 professionals worldwide in fifteen overlapping nets of affinity or tribal groups. Within those fifteen nets, there are 177 nodes of experience where we've got people who are very specialized in organoleptic chemistry or whatever.

"There are fifteen autonomous segments that have a profit and loss statement, and are organizationally self-sufficient. They can float on their own. They have a practice, they do their 'thing,' and they're busy on that. They're embedded conceptually in this organization and they may be scattered geographically but they are organizationally self-sufficient. They've got enough work to continue their practice—like the pharmaceutical group which is busier than a hornet or like the environment assurance center which is dealing with post-Bhopal-type things.

"Since they float in this kind of Sargasso Sea of professionals, they find it easy to communicate not only by Telex and computer, but also by walking into the bathroom or the lunchroom or the hall. You can see people. It's just like being in the Pentagon, you can go around. That's pretty important.

"There's no single paramount leader who can control any one of those networks, because they're a bunch of *prima donnas*. They may have an organizational section head or president of a subsidiary who has a hierarchical role for administrative purposes but he or she is there not only for business administration purposes but because of peer respect.

It's a professional peer group, where the leader is sort of the 'chief of the department of surgery'."

Benzenoid snowflakes

"These centralized constellations of people can be depicted metaphorically in what I call a 'benzenoid snowflake' form. The benzene ring represents the organizational unit, the node, and the spines are the practice areas of expertise. Dots around the spine are the number of peer qualified individuals within each one of those spines.

"Underneath the professional operations is a group of senior people. They're senior gurus who look over these particular groups which are the benzene rings, so to speak. But these groups are all very fluid—we do this to satisfy the accounting aspects.

"We put all of the benzene rings together into metanets. The chemical estate with twelve people rotates and meets in the center. All of the snowflakes are floating around and melting and reforming in different crystals. It's just an interesting way to describe the organization and one way in which we network.

"Nobody really believes all of the analogy but it's more or less true. The metanets meet once a month and we talk about what's going on that might be of interest to other people. We just verbally network.

"There are about eight different metanets in the areas of life sciences, telecommunications, environmental health and safety. They are evanescent; they are dissipating structures; they're reforming. People move from one to another depending on their professional background. They're reformed depending on the market. At the same time, we have to keep track of people's contract work, and people's salaries, so they all fall within conventional classical organization. They belong to a sectional unit or a subsidiary.

"We have multiple forms. Some groups are subsidiaries, some people float in a kind of corporate cloud and are called on as independent consultants."

Preaching, practice and profit

"For example, let's take the Arthur D. Little Management Education Institute (ADLMEI), which is in the education business. This is the only place in the world that you can get an accredited master's degree in developing world management and in which the organization operates at a profit. We have a thesis that if we're going to educate in management, we ought to be able to manage it so that we break even, so we don't have to be subsidized.

"It bears on this point of networking. The ADL Institute is run separately, with separate trustees. They network by drawing on people who are working on ADL research and case work elsewhere. The Institute has an administrative staff and a dean, but the faculty is not tenured. They're contracted for the institute from the professional staff.

"We don't allow anybody to devote full time to it because we don't think that is proper for a school that teaches management practice. One becomes too theoretical. They'll come to you [gesturing toward Jeff Stamps] and say, 'Dr Stamps, we want you to talk on systems theory to this group. Will you teach a class one hour a week during this period?' You have to be pedagogically approved. We say, 'You can't preach unless you practice.' So they'd buy your services at the billing rate that you'd sell it out as a consultant and you'd teach that class. And you'd fall under the regular constraints of school—academic parameters instead of a consulting group.

"The students are people that have undergraduate degrees from the London School of Economics, or universities in Nigeria or Beirut. They are mainly from the developing world. The current class is about sixty people from two dozen nations, and a few people from the developed world who are going to work or live in the developing world. It's an eleven-and-a-half-month course which costs as much as the Harvard Business School or Sloan School of Management. All work is done by case study and lectures on activities in developing countries, and taught by consultants who are practicing in the developing countries.

"So the cases that we study are not General Motors or Volvo or Texas Instruments, but we talk about what do we do in

Mauritania? How do you operate in Tanzania if the telephones may not work? And how do you teach marketing? It's tailored to equipping these people to go back, either in industry, in education, or in government positions. They may go back as subministers or ministers. We have many distinguished government officials who've come to ADLMEI.

"The graduation ceremony is like the United Nations. We put up a tent and some attend wearing tribal dress and bring their families. It's a fantastic event."

Professionalism and integrity

Jessica and Jeff: "What is the substance of ADL? What holds your organization together?"

Bob Mueller: "Professionalism. In the sense of a high degree of integrity and concern for the ADL mission in life, which is to be 'on the leading edge of change', and to do things that are worthwhile but for a profit. We add that, realizing that we work for not-for-profit organizations. We say we ought to be able to earn a profit as a measure of the utility of what we do. We should pay our way, not be subsidized. Our major competitors who are as diversified as ADL—RAND Corporation, SRI, Battelle—do their work in the laboratory and in offices, as we do. However those are not-for-profit organizations.

"We believe we should be 'for profit,' and we add to that that we should be publicly held—at least a portion. About 71 per cent of our stock is now held in a trust fund which is for the benefit of the employees and 9 percent is in an employees' investment fund. About 20 percent is traded on NASDAQ. We say, and this is a philosophical argument at all times, that we ought not to operate as a closed corporation, which tends to function like a private partnership.

"If you satisfy a partnership you can exist as long as the partners reproduce themselves, if you will. A closed system, a partnership or privately held corporation, may not be as responsive to social and general needs as an open system, a public corporation.

"So we have to satisfy the independent investor who invests in Arthur D. Little and doesn't care whether we're working on something exciting or not. He or she invests because of the return on the investment. As long as the owners of a privately held corporation satisfy themselves and operate responsibly, in their own judgment, there isn't any way to enforce the 'ethic of service' except by statutory or regulatory means. This ethic is not as preserved as it is when you have to earn your keep for somebody who's investing in you because you make a profit while serving in the public interest.

"We're in both public and private worlds and we stay in both, a situation that's constantly under discussion and review. Some of the staff would much rather just do their thing and be paid appropriately and not have to worry about having to earn a dividend for somebody who invests in them.

"It puts a different cutting edge on remaining flexible and responsive to the market place. If it sells, fine. If it doesn't, then you change. Working for profit forces you to change because you have to stay alive.

"All that heritage, value system and belief in the sense of what is important (and some myths) wrap up into a symbol of Arthur D. Little's role in life. This is basically a role perception by the staff, and it changes as the staff changes.

"The board of directors has a role in the sense of governing, but it's difficult because we're so diversified. All they can do is to preserve the objectives, performance, reputation and the attractiveness of ADL as a place to work. The fact that we do things of which we are proud, and that our ethics and our integrity and our value to the world are recognized, earns our way.

"Perhaps that's why 2000 people send in unsolicited résumés to ADL every month. We answer all of them. We induce turnover because it brings new brains into the network. New intellectual property is added to the pot. People who have new backgrounds can come in and can sell their services either directly outside or indirectly to someone else on the staff who has a client. So you're always in the selling mode and you have to earn your keep by offering your intellectual property.

"Some staff find that uncomfortable because it is fuzzy, because it's tenuous, because the peer pressure is terrific, in a civilized way. Anything you propose can be immediately shot at.

"But the freedom to fail and the freedom to get shot at are expected. It's nothing personal, it's just an intellectual sort of a philosophy of trying to do something and innovate and implement. Those are all abstractions, but what it really boils down to is what you have to offer that is different from the many other consulting firms.

"We're always in a state of change. That's why this depiction is a snapshot. It's moving. It's like looking at an aquarium with things moving. Occasionally the sharks get over in one corner together, and the jellyfish get over here and the sunfish get over here. Pretty soon they all move around and they re-sort themselves."

Trust that binds

"Movement goes on all the time here and the main thing that holds the organization together is trust and respect between individuals. These are the elements that you two have written about so eloquently. The empowerment of networks and the reason they're cemented together is personal trust and respect. That exists here. If it doesn't exist, then it doesn't fly.

"This doesn't mean that everyone networks with everyone else. It's like any other human group. It's not all one happy family, you know; there are little families, little groups. It's like any civilization, small community, or society. It's a society of its own with different pockets of completely opposite attitudes. It's all held together by superlative ethics.

"Most of the things that we do have the potential, or perception of such, of a conflict of interest in some way. There is an opportunity to mishandle inside information. Every professional on the staff knows the code of ethics here, which is not only written but is constantly reinforced. If we misbehave in that regard, we don't last. So it's self-correcting in that way.

"The network is based on a trust and a high intellectual respect for the sanctity of information and deciding what is in the public domain and what is not. We've got cases here that we work on where we're working on security information and only a few know what's underway. And we don't work on projects for two different governments or

43

companies if there's a potential for strategic conflict. We are very careful about that and we turn down business because of that.

"We can be working for one company that's trying to acquire another and we can't get tangled up in that. We stay away from executive recruiting. Some consulting firms do recruiting. But if a client ever thought that we had identified somebody who relocated because of knowledge of their staff, we'd get really zapped. So we stay away entirely from recruiting as a professional practice.

"These potential conflicts are essentially managed by individuals. There's no one person or one group who can effectively manage all interrelationships or intervene or listen in on the network communications.

"For example, I don't know what a person is doing unless I'm working with him or her. So it's an interesting way to work as opposed to an industrial hierarchical organization where the boss knows what the people below are doing. You are expected to tell the superior what you are doing. As a result the information flow can get constrained."

Jessica and Jeff: "You had many years in a different kind of organization. What brought you to this view? Or did it come to you when you came to ADL?"

Bob Mueller: "It came to me when I came to ADL. I worked thirty-three years in hierarchy—board, executive committee and chairman roles. I came here to do consulting, writing and some lecturing, because one of the officers at my former place of employment had become an officer here and said, 'Come on over here because we have more fun.'

"I never knew what happiness was until I got into the consulting world and then it was too late, you might say! You lose a lot of the perks, privileges, and trappings of power which many, many hierarchical positions have.

CHAPTER 4

Caretakers of the planet

Human beings are now confronted with the
fact that we share a planet together. . . . No
matter what else we may be, we are also *planet*
people, part of the Earth's living biosphere.
Planet Drum Foundation

In the landmark film *The Powers of Ten*, one of the finest attempts
to help people understand the levels of natural organization, the
viewer is taken on a journey that begins with a person lying on a
beach, continues outward up a series of steps through the solar
system to the theoretical edge of the universe, returns to the person
on the beach and then descends a staircase through the body to
the lilliputian world of the electron.

It is absolutely mind-boggling to try to grasp the ideas of the
vastness of the universe and the minuteness of the electron at the
same time. In the middle of the macro/microcosm is the person,
the zero point for all human-comprehensible scales of large and
small. Complementing the unique perspective of one person is the
singular whole that encompasses us all, our one earth. The meaning
that author Theodore Roszak has telescoped into the phrase
"person/planet" [the title of one of his books] is represented by
the astronaut circling the moon and emotionally exclaiming, "I can
hold the earth in the palm of my hand." Each of us does, indeed,
hold that fragile jewel in the cup of our hands.

From our perspective here at the computer, we find it difficult
to remember that we are just tiny specks on the planet, two of the
now four and a half billion people who populate the 10 percent
of the earth on which people live (about a person for each year of
our planet's evolution). That recognition of the interconnectedness

of everything, an ancient truth of many religions, gives rise to a vast network that girds the globe, linking climatologists with local environmentalists, horticulturalists with corporate CEOs, peasants with princes.

Ever since the 1962 publication of Rachel Carson's terrifying book *Silent Spring*, which revealed the impact of chemical pollution on our rivers, streams and oceans, networks have been forming around the ideas of clean environments, ecological balance, the responsible use of the earth's resources, creating technologies that are life-enhancing and in proportion to what author Kirkpatrick Sale has identified as *human scale* in his book by that name. These networks appear to be singularly adept at holding together and celebrating the incredible powers of the earth to provide us with everything from grapes and electricity to yurts and flight to whales and rainbows.

Were it not for the oddly forgettable fact that everything *is* interconnected, the exploitation of natural resources might have been relegated to a list of concerns that could be dealt with later. However, what "the caretakers of the planet" tell us is that we have to change our patterns of resource consumption and develop new resources or be prepared to die on a desolate, barren, spoiled planet. We cannot strip the Black Hills of South Dakota without disturbing the ecology of the entire region and ultimately the world. Nor can we ignore the question, what is nature's response to the decimation of whole species, whether tiny snail darters or gargantuan whales? According to some ecologists, the November 1985 "volcano eruption" in Colombia was actually a mud slide aggravated by soil erosion due to improper planting of coffee bushes—which could have been planted ecologically.

Chroniclers throughout history have documented the development of humanity's mastery over resources—from the Prometheus legend that describes him stealing fire from the gods to matriarchical studies (such as that of Elizabeth Gould Davis) which credit women with the discovery of tools and fire. Fire, one of nature's gifts, illustrates how such gifts may be *used* or *abused*. Fire can be used constructively for cooking, heating and lighting, but it can also be awesomely destructive. As entrepreneurs dismantle whole mountain ranges in order to turn shale into coal and coal into gas, the abuse of gifts hundreds of millions of years in the making seems staggering.

Because the term "resource use" itself has a connotative tinge of exploitation, it reminds us that virtually all ecological/energy choices have harmful side effects or are restricting to someone or something. As "*sapiens*", we are not yet wise enough to fully grasp the ramifications of our personal and social choices as they relate to the bioplanet. As inhabitants of the Invisible Planet, we strive to do the best we can, acting more like "caretakers" than "visitors"—which is how the Community Congress of San Diego describes itself:

> "Caretaker" is a term used by Edward E. Sampson to describe those individuals who value and care for the earth they live on, the people they live with, and the other life forms which surround them. Sampson contrasts "caretakers" with "visitors" who when visiting different locations stop long enough to exploit the territory, taking things of value and leaving their cast-off debris and garbage.

Environment

The environmental movement got its start in the US in the 1950s and 1960s when outdoor adventurers caught wind of the fact that developers were moving in on their territory. Born principally as a network of concern among mountain climbers, backpackers, bird watchers, and other nature lovers, these people began to coordinate their efforts and eventually joined long-standing outdoor recreation organizations such as the Sierra Club to work around conservation issues.

With roots reaching back to the turn of the century, the Sierra Club is the grandparent of the early conservation movement. (The Sierra Club headquarters in San Francisco was one of only two buildings to survive that city's 1906 earthquake.) During the Depression, the Sierra Club was the leader in a number of conservation battles, opposing such outrageous plans as a federal government scheme to flood the Grand Canyon and turn it into a lake!

Before long, conservation became too narrow a term to describe the problem: the issues went much deeper than the felling of redwoods for the purpose of building highways. As the conservation movement gathered steam, so was a parallel group concerned with the quality of air. "In 1964," writes futurist Hazel

Henderson in her book *Creating Alternative Futures: The End of Economics*, "I joined with some other worried citizens and mothers of small children in New York City to form an organization called Citizens for Clean Air. I soon learned that if the air was to remain breathable and the environment life-sustaining for my infant daughter during her lifetime, I and other citizens would have to commit ourselves to a process of learning about the complex, interdependent, urban industrial societies in which we lived and about the basic assumptions on which their technical and economic systems were founded."

For a number of years, the two branches of the movement remained separate. Henderson recalls writing to conservation-oriented environmentalists in the early 1960s, asking if they were concerned with urban environmental issues such as air pollution and lead contamination. She was shocked when the reply came back: "We see no connection."

Eventually, however, the rural conservationists and the urban environmentalists did meet, and over the next few years Henderson-type thinking attracted a large, committed following that worked on many local environmental issues, culminating in the first national environmental action in the US, in 1970. On 22 April of that year, people with these broader environmental concerns came together to celebrate Earth Day in Washington, DC, and sites throughout the US. Earth Day attracted tremendous media attention: The image of the earth as a brilliant blue-and-white-swirled ball hanging in black space became a widely recognized symbol, and before long "ecology," a word previously reserved for biology classes, became commonly used.

Ecology and a clean environment have great appeal. It's difficult to find anyone who will consciously speak against clean air or clean rivers. Yet, being in favor of clean air and doing something about it are two quite different matters. Out of the large inactive network of implicit environmental concerns have arisen a number of action-oriented groups working in different ways to preserve the planet and its many levels of physical, biological, and human complexity.

Breaking off from the Sierra Club in the late 1960s, Friends of the Earth (FOE) serves as a cornerstone of the environmentalist movement. One of the largest groups currently active in the movement, FOE has evolved into an activist environmental lobby, working on legislation and mounting public campaigns around such issues as nuclear power, clean energy, clean air, wild lands, and wildlife. FOE also maintains contacts with independent sister groups in twenty-three other countries.

FOE's greatest impact may be a few years in the future, as the innovative ideas of physicist Amory Lovins, once FOE's London representative, and his wife lawyer Hunter Lovins, receive wider publicity and are actively applied. Working from their passive solar Rocky Mountain Institute, the Lovinses have put forth their plan for "a route to reliance half a century from now based solely on renewable energy sources—solar energy and its derivatives, including wind and water power, and the conversion of organic matter into fuels. Energy conservation and frugal use of fossil fuels will get us through the transition period," Friends of the Earth literature explains.

One of the Lovinses' greatest achievements may be in persuading people who are deeply committed to preserving "wilderness" to recognize the interconnectedness of open space and the greater issues of how we are going to use all our resources.

"Wilderness is a strictly civilized concept," says Roger Dunsmore in *Wild Idea . . . Wild Hope*, a pamphlet published by Planet Drum Foundation. "The fact that we see natural areas as 'wild' and call them wilderness is an indication of the extent to which we are removed from our own natural state. It must be completely unimaginable to indigenous people that we could call their life-sphere a 'wild' place. Wilderness is a home. It's a home for whatever species are there and it's the original human home."

Planet Drum publishes a variety of innovative materials about different "regions" of the planet. Unrestricted by form or content, Planet Drum gathers together whatever it needs in the way of material to understand a region of the earth, transforms it into resplendently designed media—which include, variously, maps, charts, poems, diaries, newsletters, and essays—calls it a "bundle," and mails it off to members.

A bundle from Planet Drum on the Rocky Mountains called "Backbone—The Rockies" includes a conversation between the group's review (*Raise the Stakes!*) editor, Peter Berg, and goehistorian Robert Curry; "Rockies—The Source," a study compiled by residents of the Slocan Valley, in British Columbia; "Rocky Mountain lifetime," an amazing information wheel about the region; "A house at 8000," a journal excerpt about life in a solar-heated house in the Rockies; *Wild Idea . . . Wild Hope*, the pamphlet mentioned above; and "The eye in the rock," a poem celebrating the beauty and spirit of the Rockies. A beautiful map delineates the spine of the Rockies from north of the Peace River and east of Slave Lake, in the Canadian Northwest Territories, to the valley carved out in the southwestern United States between the Colorado and the Rio Grande and carries this description:

> Think of the Rocky Mountains as a sunburst or a star. Its rays are patterns of water and soil moving across North America. Soil fertility from the cornfields of Indiana to the delta of the Columbia in Oregon is owed to nutrients eroded from the Rockies by wind and water.
>
> People in the Rockies live in the heart of the star. People living in the Mississippi Delta, on the edges of the Bering Sea and the Gulf of California, around the Hudson Bay, people at the far reaches of the rays, all watch Rockies water go by.

When we saw the Rockies in this pattern, we knew that we had yet another image of a network to add to our mental collection.

Eco-consciousness (ecological consciousness), such as that purveyed by Planet Drum, is mind-expanding; it transcends national borders, legislative actions, and economic gaming. "There is adequate new evidence for considering the Rockies as a whole and continuous biotic province or biogeographical province: a neutral natural zone whose real survival is based on biological and geological processes rather than on the priorities of nations, states, or provinces, and corporations whose boundaries and self-interests run willy-nilly throughout the region."

Whereas one stream of the environmental movement works at the legislative and regulatory level (such as FOE and Environmental Action) and a second stream works to network information (such as Planet Drum), yet a third stream of the movement is focused on action.

Greenpeace, an international direct action environmental organization, has engaged in some of the most dramatic and effective campaigns to protect the planet and its denizens in this century. "We attempt to spotlight ecological atrocities by nonviolent physical protest at the scene," said former San Francisco Greenpeace Director Tom Falvey. "Thus we have placed our bodies between harpoons and endangered whales every year since 1975 in the Pacific, the Atlantic, off Australia and Japan. We go up to the Newfoundland ice floes every March (since 1976) and confront the sealers who club newborn seals to death for their pelts.

"In 1971, 1972, and 1973 we sent ships into both the American and French nuclear weapon test zones during the actual explosions(!) to interfere with, and provoke public protest against, these test runs for Armageddon." In 1985, Greenpeace made front-page headlines in newspapers around the world when its maiden vessel *Rainbow Warrior* was blown up by French secret service agents. The explosion which took the life of Fernando Pereira, a Dutch photo journalist, occurred while the ship was moored in an Auckland, New Zealand harbor, slated to sail into French nuclear test zones. The French defense minister resigned and two of the French agents were charged with and pled guilty to manslaughter.

Later in 1985, the ship *Greenpeace* sailed from New Zealand to establish a base camp in Antarctica. "The *Greenpeace* is going to claim Antarctica for all peoples of the world," explains Peter Bahouth, chair of Greenpeace USA. "We want to show that Antarctica needs to be preserved as the last unspoiled continent on the planet."

Greenpeace is a no-frills organization, distributing only that information that is directly relevant to what it is doing. Its one-page information sheets on topics such as "Of whales and whaling," "Nuclear disarmament," and "Toxics" are succinct, fact-filled statements about these problems.

The poignant image of Greenpeacers in their rubber dinghies rolling over ocean waves as they protect sea mammals from their would-be executioners is the stuff of which myths are created, material sufficient for the awe-inspiring book *Warriors of the Rainbow* by Robert Hunter. Even the names they chose, Greenpeace for the movement and *Rainbow Warrior* for the vessel, carry a planetary survival message. While soldiers have for forty centuries identified themselves with minute, arbitrarily defined patches of the earth's surface, fighting humans to "protect" humans, these terrestrial guerrillas identify with the planet as a whole, indeed, with existence as a whole, transcending human chauvinism. Greenpeace lives the belief that the planet and all its creatures are one.

Renewable energy

Nowhere is the concept of "opportunity in crisis" so clear as in the energy field. Renewable (also called "alternative") energy is the summary title for a number of initiatives—what Amory Lovins calls "the soft energy path" (see his 1977 book by that title)—or what could simply be called "the soft solar network", since all energy sources ultimately derive from the sun. For practical purposes, it is helpful to make some distinctions within the soft energy field, since each of the "paths" encompasses its own network of people and projects that interweave and exchange resources. Some of these paths are:

- The (specifically) *solar* network, the largest, best-known, and most universally applicable of our available, energy options;
- The *wood* network, growing primarily in the forest-rich, generally northern and mountainous regions;
- The *wind* network, appropriately positioned chiefly at water's edge;
- The *water* network, tapping the available power coursing by our two ocean coasts, by scores of mighty rivers, and by thousands of backwater streams that already have dams.

Along with the groups that stress the values of conservation, cogeneration (using energy ordinarily wasted in energy-conversion processes, such as drying clothes in wood-stove-warmed rooms), and waste conversion (such as is involved in the production of methane gas), these organic, noninvasive, self-renewing energy networks stand in sharp contrast to the fossil-fuel industries, which were born of a worldview in which more is better, waste creates profit, side effects are trivialized, and the past (fossil) and future be damned. Even the names of these abundant resource networks sun, wood, wind, and water—have an elemental poetry about them.

Obtaining our energy by deliberately digging into the earth with mines and wells instead of receiving it with open arms directly from the sun makes us look like ridiculous energy ostriches. What could be better than obtaining our energy from the sun—our boundless, inexhaustible, everlasting, completely free local furnace? Perhaps the greatest obstacle to solar energy exists not in the technology to tap it, which ranges from absolutely nothing to sophisticated photovoltaic storage cells, but rather, in the fact that no one can own the sun. Unlike the moon that America planted old Glory upon, the sun eludes ownership. Imagine affixing the American flag, or as has been done with most of our other natural resources, a corporate logo, to the sun.

The solar network has been by far the most effective, even though precariously balanced and potentially threatened, of all the grids in the renewable-energy field. Perhaps because solar-generated heat and power are so potentially competitive with their fossil-fuel rivals, the solar solution has been back-burnered, budget-cut, and research-reported nearly to death. Yet solar energy is a practical, economical, available technology that could be put into place almost overnight. Indeed, the slogan of the nuclear power industry, "safe, clean, and cheap," by rights belongs to the sun. In three stunning pages in *Human Scale*, Kirkpatrick Sale summarizes the solar argument. Using such concepts as economical, conservational, democratic, decentralized, efficient, and adaptable, Sale demonstrates that solar technology is the appropriate energy source for now and the future, consistent with the needs and values of the Invisible Planet.

The use of wood for energy began hundreds of thousands of years ago and has continued unabated to the present. In Third and Fourth World countries, wood is at the basis of both survival and ritual. A typical family in western Africa spends 20–30 percent of its income on firewood; in Thailand, a father's role at his child's birth is to keep the fire burning with special wood he has gathered during the ninth month of pregnancy. Wood may have lost some of this traditional magic in America, but its use is on the rise, with about 1.5 million households having converted to wood in the 1980 season alone and an estimated 15 million households heating with wood in 1985. The smell of burning apple wood and the quiet heat of the fire, coupled with independence from expensive and noisy oil-powered systems, draw people to heating with wood. Publications such as *Wood N' Energy*, the newsletter of the Society for the Protection of New Hampshire Forests, and the *Wood Burning Quarterly*, in Minnesota, keep wood burners up to date on the latest tips and developments. However, one of the more sobering developments was the quick realization by wood-stove manufacturers and users that this form of combustion is a heavy pollutant itself. Hazel Henderson states the problem frankly:

> Wood-burning is becoming a significant air pollution problem releasing many carcinogens, particulates, *and* Dioxin (as in Agent Orange). New England wood-stove romanticism is about finished. All stoves are polluters and will have to be redesigned or retrofitted.

Similarly, wind power is hardly a universal panacea for energy generation; yet, in the appropriate location, wind is both sensible and economical. On Cuttyhunk Island, off the southern coast of Massachusetts, for example, a single windmill is supplying half the electric requirements for the island, not an inconsiderable reduction in a community dependent on the importation of diesel fuel by barge that has driven the local utility rates 20 percent higher than those of New York City. But even that unlikely spot, New York City, is the home of a commercial scale windmill, built by local teenagers, and now supplying all the electricity to an apartment building on the city's Lower East Side.

Clearly, windpower is on the upswing, and although the US wind industry is a distant relative of our travelogue image of Holland's windmills, "the winds, they are a'blowing" with the promise of locally generated power.

The potential for hydroelectric power generation is great and widespread. Dams need not be the size of the gargantuan Bonneville Dam, in Washington, or require bureaucracies the size of the Tennessee Valley Authority, to generate electricity. Literally thousands of rural river runs are rushing water past people blind to the power available to them. In New England alone, more than 250 sites are under consideration for development of hydro-generated power.

Recognizing the potential in our riverways, as well as in the oceans themselves, water-generated-power groups have been spreading the word about this nonpolluting form of energy. "Most of the nation's water potential is unused, but enough unused back-country dams exist in the US *right now*, according to the Federal Power Commission, to supply the entire annual electrical needs for a population of 40 million people—more than the Rocky Mountain and Pacific regions combined—if only they were equipped with generators," writes Sale. While most of the projects are being developed by renewable-resource-minded entrepreneurs, support for water power comes through conservation groups concerned with other issues, as well as from industry groups such as the National Alliance for Hydroelectric Energy, based in Washington.

Sun, wood, wind, water—the sources of power for human civilization since its origin. An inventive spirit motivates the reclaiming of these power sources for future human civilization, a spirit which merges often with the creative forces behind appropriate technology.

Appropriate technology

Small Cat, a wise old ancestor, sat on the windowsill, basking in the sun. "But she's not small," people would say when they asked her name. "She may not be small," we replied, "but she is beautiful."

Our cat's name is one of many fanciful, affectionate uses to which the name of the famous book by the late British economist E. F. Schumacher has been put. *Small Is Beautiful* introduced people to the idea of the human side of technology, of tools that could be seen as *appropriate* to living in harmonious balance with the earth.

Appropriate technology has had as many descriptions as it has had applications, ranging from very fuzzy notions of sometimes crazy-looking contraptions to more generalized, value-oriented definitions such as the one offered by the Southern Unity Network/Renewable Energy Project (SUN/REP): "Appropriate technology is any technology—old or new—which is decentralized, labor-intensive, small-scale, accessible to rich and poor, and safe."

Appropriate technology conjures up images of windmills, waterwheels, compost heaps, organic gardens, wood stoves, solar panels and bicycles. For those who have made the study and invention of appropriate technologies their life work, the concept embraces many kinds of tools that people can use on a human scale. Appropriate technology has broad appeal in a world in which people are overwhelmed by buildings that are so tall that they sway in the wind, by planes that fly so far overhead that we only hear them, and by traffic that becomes so jammed at the end of the workday that people can actually *save* time by *waiting* to leave until rush hour is over. Appropriate technology is based on the decentralized use of tools in contrast to that overapplied informing principle of industrial civilization: centralization. Centralization has rendered many institutions, services, and approaches ineffective, frustrating, unresponsive, and alienating, by making them too big and too abusive of critical balances.

With the awareness that locally originated and point-to-point services are often the most sensible means of solving local technical problems, the appropriate technology movement has been strongly attracted to the idea of networking. Indeed, among the first groups to create networks in the 1970s were the AT centers, and, unlike other networks that have chosen words such as "movement," "group," "association" and sundry other nouns to sum up their collectivity, nearly all the AT groups have at some time called themselves or one of their offshoots a "network."

One of the first and longest-standing AT initiatives is *Rain Magazine*. Begun in 1974 as a newsletter for sharing AT information in the Pacific Northwest, the Portland-based publication now enjoys international readership. The magazine quickly brings the reader up to date on what's happening in AT; each issue includes book reviews, "how to's," excerpts from reports, interviews, essays, and short new blurbs. *Rain* has also given birth to several books (notably *The Rainbook*) and to primers on various subjects.

By the mid-1970s, the *Rain* office had become one of the highlights of the AT circuit, attracting everyone from college students doing term papers on AT to governors and corporate executives. As success is often measured in notoriety, it could be said that AT efforts had met with tremendous success. This success produced an identity crisis of sorts in the AT community, one that typically faces successful networks. A January 1980 essay in the "Raindrops" column of *Rain* sums up the predicament:

Appropriate technology, whether called that or not, has been receiving increased recognition and gaining national and international prominence as a key component in the transition to a more ecologically and socially balanced world. At the same time, the recent whirlwind of attention has precipitated a kind of "growth" in appropriate technology not unlike the "growth" we've been discussing the limits of for so many years—an undifferentiated, somewhat out-of-control growth that's happening so far and so wide and so fast it seems nearly impossible to keep track of until it's already become history.

One thing we've learned from the "limits of growth" debate is that "growth", like "development," is a word with many connotations. As far as the growth of appropriate technology, we have to ask *what kind of growth* are we working toward? And further, *what kind of movement* should the appropriate technology movement become?

There are hard questions to be answered. What does it mean after being on the outside for all these years to find ourselves on the inside? What does it mean to have a surge of public attention, corporate interest and government support (though still a piddling amount when compared to things like nuclear power and defense) on our work toward local self-reliance? Some pretty important distinctions are getting blurred—do we need to draw the line?

AT projects are numerous and inspiring, and visits to some experimental centers are like time travel into Utopia. New implementations of R. Buckminster Fuller's famous phrase "doing more with less" are being developed at locations such as the Farallones Integral Urban House, in Berkeley, California—where rabbits replace lawn mowers and garbage disposals take the form of sawdust buckets. At the New Alchemy Institute in Falmouth, Massachusetts, fish are farmed in indoor solar-heated pools. Such sophisticated and beautiful projects could be called appropriate *art*. Adaptations of these ideas are being tried elsewhere as the AT network reaches from the high-tech United States to the jungles of Guatemala to the food-short nations of Africa.

One international node in the AT movement is in a tiny village in the mountains of Maine, barely twenty miles from the Canadian border. It is from Rangeley, Maine, that TRANET, the Transnational Network for Appropriate/Alternative Technologies, conducts its business.

TRANET got its start at the 1976 HABITAT Forum of the UN Conference on Human Settlements, in Vancouver, Canada, and has grown to be a membership organization of 1200, exchanging information with nearly 500 magazines, newsletters and journals, and maintaining files on 1500 AT or "new age" groups and 10,000 names and addresses of interested individuals. This organization is known primarily through its quarterly newsletter/directory, an excellent distillation of information about activities and articles relevant to its membership.

"A network has no center," TRANET coordinator/executive director William Ellis, a no-nonsense former physician born as the fifth generation Ellis in Rangeley, told us at the start of our conversation. Hence, a network does not need imposing facilities and urban amenities. "I inherited this house, where I was born, from my parents. And this is where our family is practicing self-reliant living. We grow our own food, cut our own wood, and have fitted our house with solar collectors. We feel that if we espouse self-reliance, we should practice it. The only time we drive the car is to take our useless garbage—mostly plastic to the dump."

Having just returned from one of his frequent trips around the world, on which he had spent time with "UN and government bureaucrats who talk appropriate technology from their high-life-style penthouses." Ellis was nonetheless feeling very optimistic. "Five years ago, the Nepalese Government thought that 'appropriate technology' was really our second-hand stuff. Now they understand what AT is all about, and they're eager to learn what's happening in Guatemala, in Africa, wherever."

For Ellis, Rangeley, Maine, is a perfect spot from which to reach around the globe. "Most of our international work is done by telephone, and the communications system here, the phones and the mail, are excellent. In fact, the phone service and mail is probably better here than it is in New York."

Beyond its valuable information services, TRANET is also developing and espousing a philosophy of transnationalism grounded in networking. "AT goes way beyond windmills and conservation and cutting your own wood, way beyond the hardware and the software," Ellis says. "AT has also to do with the way our world is organized, which is why we have formed a network" (see Chapter 10).

TRANET's unfolding ideas about our preparation as global people to leap beyond national boundaries are presented in the Fall 1979 newsletter in a short essay, "A second level of world governance":

Nation-states have governed world affairs for only a very brief period of human history. These autonomous governmental bodies have divided the land of the earth into a crazy-quilt chess board with little concern for culture, languages, religions, races, or ecologies. Both within and between these meaningless boundaries weird games of politics are played with the resources and lives of people. It is time to ask to what extent this world governmental system is to be changed if we are to reach the full potential of human development. . . .

People in all parts of the world are recognizing that big business, big government, big technology, and other centralized organizations cannot alone solve local problems or develop local potentials, only the people themselves can. And, people in all parts of the world are recognizing not only that small is beautiful but also that small is possible and small is happening. There is a worldwide revival of human rights, human dignity, and individual initiative. . . . This decade may be hailed as the beginning of the future because people-to-people networks initiated a more creative approach to world welfare—a complementary alternative to the UN—a second level of world governance.

Toward which end TRANET is working. In 1981, TRANET initiated the first of its people-to-people exchanges through its Associates Program in which skilled technical people from AT groups in one part of the world make three-month site visits to AT groups in another part of the world, an idea that Ellis believes has its long-time precedents in the international Sister Cities program (Boston, Massachusetts, and Kyoto, Japan, for example) and the US-based Experiment in International Living, which sponsors high school student exchanges.

Even TRANET's governing-board structure reflects its philosophy. Its twenty-five board members come from five geographic regions: Africa (presently represented with directors from Ghana, Senegal, Nigeria and Tanzania); Asia and the Pacific (India, Pakistan, Papua New Guinea and Indonesia); Latin America (Colombia, Mexico, Ecuador, Guatemala and Chile); Europe and the Middle East (the Netherlands, England, France, Iran and Switzerland); and North America (United States and Canada). Further, the annual meetings are rotated among the continents as is the presidency.

The developing TRANET philosophy is somewhat reminiscent

of the original vision proposed for world government, prior to Woodrow Wilson's League of Nations scheme. Early UN, or perhaps more accurately, world-union, ideas put professional associations (potentially representing the whole range of people's interests) on an equal footing with nation-state governments. Had this idea become reality, the world union might now be according equal importance to national governments and the worldwide nongovernmentally indentured networks of windmill builders, of midwives, of poets. A dream, perhaps, but. . . .

CHAPTER 5

Struggles for the basics

Almost 300 years ago, in the then "new world," local groups calling themselves Committees of Correspondence formed a network, a communications forum where homespun political and economic thinkers hammered out their ideological differences, sculpting the form of a separate and independent country in North America. Writing to one another and sharing letters with neighbors, this revolutionary generation nurtured its adolescent ideas into a mature politics. Both men and women participated in the debate over independence from England and the desirable shape of the American future. It was in one of these letters that Abigail Adams first mentioned the idea of enfranchisement for women, while another of her friends, the playwright Mercy Otis Warren, used ideas from the letters to create her popular political satires about the British.

During the years in which the American Revolution was percolating, letters, newssheets and pamphlets carried from one village to another were the means to refine ideas about democracy. In time, the correspondents agreed to hold a face-to-face meeting. The concepts of independence and government had been debated, discussed, discarded and reformulated literally hundreds of times by the time people in the revolutionary network met in Philadelphia.

After the writers met in a series of conferences and worked out a statement of purpose, which they called a "Declaration of Independence," the network of correspondence and printed broadsides led to the formation of an organization. Did our early networking grandparents realize that the result of their youthful idealism, less than two centuries later, would be a global superpower with an unparalleled ability to influence the survival of life on the planet?

Like stars and people, governments are born, grow and die. Their life cycles are punctuated by transitions and upheavals, patterns found in the development of all complex physical, biological and human entities. Just as we humans are evolving, so are our politics—our social forms, our collective associations— evolving. As we evolve, so do our ideas about possible political structures. There is no name for it yet, this politics of the future.

In a letter to Samuel Kercheval written on 12 July 1816, Thomas Jefferson expressed his long-held belief that each generation has a right and a duty to re-agree upon the fundamental laws by which it is governed, to reassess the laws of nature as they are presently understood.

> Some men look at constitutions with sanctimonious reverence and deem them like the arc of the covenant, too sacred to be touched. . . . But I know that laws and institutions must go hand in hand with the progress of the human mind. As [the mind] becomes more developed, more enlightened, as new discoveries are made, new truths disclosed, and manners and opinions change with the change of circumstances, institutions must advance also and keep pace with the times. . . . Let us [not] weakly believe that one generation is not as capable as another of taking care of itself and of ordering its own affairs. . . . Each generation is as independent of the one preceding as that was of all which had gone before. It has then, like them, a right to choose for itself the form of government it believes most promotive of its own happiness, consequently, to accommodate to the circumstances in which it finds itself that received from its predecessors.

Not only constitutions but also our declarations about the fundamental laws of nature are not sacred absolutes of human knowledge. Our covenants about what is real and how reality works have already undergone radical revisions a number of times in human history. To paraphrase Jefferson's view: every generation has the right and the duty to reassess and re-agree upon the perceived laws of nature by which its worldview is governed. The way to our vision of a peaceful and humane planet will be by means of a substantial reordering of our shared worldview, of our shared basic assumptions and values. Only if hundreds of millions of people, in their daily lives and work, use a new worldview to create new approaches and new solutions will we survive and evolve.

Pallas Athena, the Greek goddess of wisdom, is said to have sprung fully armed and fully grown from the brow of Zeus. Proponents of gradual change sometimes use this myth to disparage proponents of radical change. Athena's story is surely a myth, because, they assert, change starts gradually and accumulates, rather than appearing full-blown overnight. Yet there is an important truth in the Athena story that is particularly applicable to changes in politics, economics and ways of knowing. Gradualists are correct in stating that social change starts with brief flickers and flashes of anomalies, exceptions, crises and lonely protesting voices that slowly gather strength and influence, but when the shift to a new worldview comes, it does so swiftly and suddenly. Since most people are blind to the precursors of fundamental change, the new wisdom seems to burst forth suddenly, fully formed and ready to address the myriad crises of the present. It's the ostrich syndrome. If your head is buried, how can your eyes see?

In our present collective drama, this moment has not yet occurred, nor is it preordained in our script of the future. None of us need be reminded of the gloomy forecasts for tomorrow's social health and personal welfare and for the planet's headlong plunge toward ecological catastrophe. Nor can we deny the dominant American sentiment as expressed by Ronald Reagan's remarkable electoral landslides in 1980 and 1984. However, scattered among the daily doomsday reports there are unmistakable signals of hidden trends that suggest the possibility of a future large-scale shift in worldviews.

One chronicler of these social signals is Alvin Toffler who asserts that the industrial worldview reached its zenith in the mid-1950s and that a "third wave" of human civilization has been building for the past twenty-five years. That is, right now the world is undergoing a transformation as significant as the shifts from hunting to agriculture at the dawn of human civilization ("first wave") and from agriculture to industry four centuries ago ("second wave"). Toffler characterizes the "hidden code" of industrial-age thought in terms of six assumptions:

Standardization
Specialization
Synchronization
Concentration
Maximization
Centralization.

As an astute reporter of the-future-right-under-our-noses, Toffler describes the emerging third wave of civilization in terms that complement the waning industrial assumptions. Decentralized structures replace centralized forms, values of appropriateness challenge maximization, power and resources are dispersed to counter concentration, flexible time patterns encroach on the linear synchronization of tasks, autonomy and self-reliance break the narrow bonds of specialization, and creative processes expressing uniqueness contrast with the frozen ruts of standardization.

Another signal of change is documented by John Naisbitt's 1982 book *Megatrends*, in which he identified ten significant trends.

From	*To*
Industrial society	Information society
Forced technology	High tech/high touch
National economy	World economy
Short-term	Long-term
Centralization	Decentralization
Institutional help	Self-help
Representative democracy	Participatory democracy
Hierarchies	Networking
North	South
Either/or	Multiple option

Underlining the most widely reported trend, the shift from an industrial to an information society, we first learned of Naisbitt's research in 1980 while using our computer to browse through the "Community News Conference" of the Electronic Information Exchange System (see Chapter 7).

In its "Values and Lifestyles" study for corporate clients, SRI International reports that a shift of values is taking place in a small but key segment of the population. Summarizing trends in terms of evolving symbols of success, the study says that, for a significant group of people, values are shifting "from quantity toward quality, from the group toward the individual, from abundance toward sufficiency and from waste toward conservation."

Past Symbols: fame, being in *Who's Who*, five-figure salary, college degree, splendid home, executive position, live-in servants, new car every year, club membership.

Present symbols: unlisted phone number, Swiss bank account, connections with celebrities, deskless office, second and third home, rare foreign car, being a vice president, being published, frequent and unpredictable world travel.

Future symbols: free time any time, recognition as a creative person, oneness of work and play, rewarded less by money than by honor and affection, major social commitments, easy laughter and unembarrassed tears, wide-ranging interests and actions, philosophical independence, loving, being in touch with oneself.

To these reports of change percolating beneath the crumbling facade of the industrial worldview can be added the rise of networks. Networks are not only the carriers of a new paradigm, they are a reflection of it: a segmented, decentralized, nonhierarchical, fuzzy, value-identified form of organization that is emerging at every social level from neighborhood to globe. The vast, vibrant, still-inchoate metanetwork of people and organizations we call the Invisible Planet is coalescing in every area of personal and social life, motivated by and bonding through shared values. Nascent therein is a great power for change.

When Americans last went to the polls to elect a President, it was 1984. 1984—this year is a fixture in our recent collective consciousness, the year in which we measured ourselves and our society against George Orwell's 1949 vision of a closed, totalitarian, technocratic society thirty-five years in the future. Now that that time-mark has passed, we can compare reality to the three governing slogans of the ruling Orwellian Party:

War Is Peace.
Freedom Is Slavery.
Ignorance Is Strength.

In a rough and premature way, the ingredients for a paradigm shift, a sudden widespread change in worldviews, are present even now. There is a vital movement for constructive change and there is as well a potentially unifying scientific philosophy forming at the frontiers of knowledge (see Chapter 10). Ironically, the Ronald Reagan years may help the people on these paths to find one another and bond into networks, generating an internal cohesion that finally creates an apparently sudden transition.

Liberalism and conservatism define the two poles of industrial politics, the former representing the layers of sophisticated patches that hold together revisionist industrialism, and the latter representing the earlier, simpler verities of classical industrialism. As long as the dynamic of decision making was locked into this pattern, only industrial alternatives could appear in the public arena. Since Reagan swept away the liberal leadership that had dominated American politics from Franklin Roosevelt's presidency, there may now be an opportunity for postindustrial alternatives to arise in counterpoint to conservative rule, generating a new, sharply defined, complementary dynamic that makes a shift possible.

Often considered the greatest of the colonial Puritan preachers, Cotton Mather was also the last. A paradigm shift is sometimes preceded by "the Cotton Mather effect," the appearance of a powerful and persuasive representative of a worldview just as it is about to be displaced. Furthermore, in evolutionary transitions, there is frequently a distinct "step-back-to-leap-forward," a reversion to earlier ideas and behaviors before a leap to a new synthesis (see Chapter 10). Ronald Reagan may prove to have been the "Cotton Mather" of the industrial worldview, and his administration a conspicuous "stepping back" before transformation in the late 1990s.

Following his sizable mandates and some early political successes, Reagan's administration had problems as the novelty wore off and the industrial crises of deficit economics, arms control, pollution and terrorism remained intractable. Since these crises are fueled by trends that are unstoppable within the industrial context, the need for a new paradigm may suddenly become intense. If a suitable conceptual vehicle is ready, then for the first time the long-submerged struggle between the old worldview and the new could burst into public consciousness.

Politics and economics are about values, about the social processes of defining, using and struggling over value.

Power and money are completely entwined in the world, and

both politics and economics relate to how we process differences in values. Capitalism is based on the assumption that profit is the single motivating economic value and that "realistic" power is devoid of human value beyond the jungle law of survival and dominance. But the citizens of the Invisible Planet understand that all power and wealth have a value context and that the evolutionary spectrum of human values is ignored only at the peril of civilization and now, perhaps, the very survival of humankind and the planet.

Networking is most evident among people who have the least power. Powerlessness is relative, and ultimately the politics/economics of "some have it, some don't" renders us all victims. In representing the range of *struggles for the basics*, we begin with a relatively small minority and gradually broaden the concept: an indigenous culture to a racial minority to grassroots activism to the women's movement to human beings everywhere threatened with species death by global catastrophe.

Indians

In 1843, the journalist Margaret Fuller (the great-aunt of R. Buck-minster Fuller) called for recognition of an indigenous people—Native Americans. Fuller recorded her thoughts in her book *Summer on the Lake*, when she visited Mackinac Island, in Lake Huron, where the Chippewa and Ottawa tribes had convened to collect their annual recompense from the American government:

> Let the missionary, instead of preaching to the Indian, preach to the trader who ruins him. . . . Let every legislator take the subject to heart, and, if he cannot undo the effects of past sin, try for that clear view and right sense that may save us from sinning still more deeply. And let every man and every woman, in their private dealings with the subjugated race, avoid all share in embittering, by insult or unfeeling prejudice, the captivity of Israel.

Fuller's sentiments can be found in many networks concerned with the preservation of indigenous cultures around the world.

Acknowledging our interconnectedness leads us to see that each of the struggles for individual and human rights is our own struggle.

Within the United States, the oldest struggle for group rights is that of Native Americans, a summary name for the 482 recognized tribes living on 266 reservations. The American government's treatment of the tribes is consistent with the raw industrial worldview in which might overrules right. White people were visitors on the land of Native Americans: had these European-descended capitalists observed their own rules concerning ownership during those early years, history would be very different.

As it was, the Indian people were "reserved" into small areas of land, mere fractions of the territory that various treaties promised. Today the struggle of the Indian peoples revolves around the land on which they live and its resources: oil, coal, uranium, gas and water—all in rich abundance on many reservations. Without land, the traditional tribal way perishes.

The factors of high alcohol and suicide rates, severely depressed income and educational levels, and the jailing of many leaders of the Indian movement have brought Native people to the verge of extinction. A strong network of support, largely invisible, exists to reverse these realities, to celebrate the great heritage of the American Indian and to pave the way for another future.

One of the oldest and most visible support groups within the movement is the National Indian Youth Council (NIYC), which addresses such issues as land and resources, tribal government, health care and anti-Indian backlash, and sponsors programs in employment, appropriate technology, youth recreation, environmental education, paralegal training, voter registration and litigation. NIYC was born as an informal network and grew by consciously understanding itself as a process.

In history and principle, the National Indian Youth Council is a process, not an event. The process began in 1952 when Indian clubs at various universities began to form regional associations. It came to fruition during the Conference on American Indians (Chicago, 1960) when non-Indian scholars discussing Indian problems invited Indians for the first time to participate in their deliberations. The well-known "Chicago Conference" had two effects: it demonstrated the absurdity of white scholars trying to define Indian problems; and the necessity for a national Indian organization to define its own problems and offer solutions consistent with Indian culture and tradition.

NIYC was created in Gallup, New Mexico, in 1961, by ten college educated Indians who had met at the Conference and envisioned that NIYC would become an organization of service to Indian People based upon the Indian system of agreement. . . . Each tribe has a distinct history; thus each tribe has different priorities in dealing with their problems and needs. What works for one tribe does not necessarily work for another tribe. NIYC approaches and responds to the variety of problems so differently that it may appear to the uninitiated that NIYC does not have a consistent philosophy or specific direction; but to NIYC this direction is as logical as the growth of a tree.

Only one of countless indigenous-culture support groups around the world, NIYC symbolizes the need for adaptive, nondogmatic networks that grow organically rather than by preordained ideology.

Blacks

Movements for social and political change in the United States began in the very process of birth of the country, which was itself such a movement. In the 1800s, the focus was on the abolition of slavery, then enfranchisement for men, while the turn of the century saw the focus shift to concern with workers' rights, immigrant "assimilation," and women's suffrage. By the 1950s, a new era was heralded with concern for civil rights for black people, a massive effort that spawned a number of other movements, including the black power movement, the anti-Vietnam War movement, and the women's movement.

But whatever happened to the civil rights movement and later the black power movement? The civil rights movement did not disintegrate with the silencing of some of its leaders by imprisonment and by death, but rather was diffused by its own internal shifting concerns. When the Rev. Martin Luther King was gunned down in Memphis, he was there to lead a march about jobs; the drive for black employment is one of many issue-related efforts that continue in the 1980s. By 1985, apartheid in South Africa held global attention.

The theory of networking suggests that the people-to-people links at the basis of the black power movement reach deep into the community, reinfusing the culture with a sense of identity.

A personal story brought this point home to us: Lucrecy Johnson is a 65-year-old American black woman, born in Creedmoor, North Carolina, who moved north in the great migration of southern blacks at the tail end of the US Depression. She raised her four children mostly alone and has had a hand in raising nearly all of a dozen grandchildren and as many great-grandchildren. She has worked all of her life, buying everything on time—even her indoor bathroom, which in 1970 was finally installed in her small wood frame house on the only unpaved street in her segregated Pennsylvania town.

Johnson eschewed the black power movement at its most media-visible height, firmly stating that she was not "black." Yet the ideas of the movement reached her. When "Roots," a second-generation offshoot of black cultural pride, was first aired on American tele-vision in the mid-1970s, Johnson was ready: her response was to dig into an old box in her attic and pull out the only existing photo of her grandmother. "I was always ashamed of this picture," she said, "because my grandmother was a slave. But now I realize who she was and that I can be proud of her." The picture now sits in her living room alongside that of her children's graduation and wedding pictures.

The black power movement separated into myriad small local action projects that have touched many aspects of people's daily lives. While the large national organizations—such as the Urban League, NAACP and PUSH—appear to be at the "head" of the black movement, a much larger, largely invisible infrastructure exists which sets up day-care centers, forms local community alliances, establishes cultural associations, involves people in tenants-rights activities, serves meals to the infirm and provides access to inner-city gardening plots.

Networking is the key to survival for all minority groups. At a time when the voices of division grow loud—pitting Black against Jew, Haitian against Cuban, Vietnamese against Chicano—it is doubly important that we work from our sense of intercon-nectedness as a species. Since greed and hate can never be the basis of lasting associations, those without power and resources must share and love. Now is a crucial time for networks to work together.

Women

The women's movement, while purportedly working on "one group's" issues, actually represents deep concern for the preservation of individual rights. The women's movement is ultimately about the power each woman assumes over her own destiny. The struggle encompasses global issues: how humanity should proceed, what values will inform our decision making, and how our decisions will be made.

One of the early recognitions of the "second wave" of feminism was that our language itself would become an issue. Historically, most women have been defined by their domestic identities and by their relationships to men: the use of gender-specific words like "mankind" as the "generic" form makes it difficult to dispel old ideas about sex roles and to avoid passing stereotypes on to our children.

Early misinterpretations of the second wave of feminism led people to believe that women "wanted to be men." While many women chose to perform tasks traditionally reserved for men, men likewise chose professions traditionally reserved for women. These role changes are not the point of the women's movement; they are merely its byproduct.

At issue to the women's movement is a fundamental change in the way men and women understand one another and cooperate in the world. The women's movement is about the integrity of individuals.

The heart and soul of the women's movement rests in networking: women making connections among women. Indeed, the entire genesis of the 1960s-born women's movement can be traced to myriad networks that spontaneously developed throughout North America and abroad. Meeting in small groups—called "consciousness raising" sessions (a term later adopted by the human potential movement)—women experienced dramatic flashes of awareness of the *Gestalt* in which they lived. These "clicks," as writer Jane O'Reilly called them, were the architecture that framed

71

the larger worldview, the personal proofs that isolated women share many problems in patriarchal society.

The women's movement is about awareness and about consciousness, concerns with profound implications for our developing human species. Its most expansive thinkers talk of an integration of political and economic issues with new ways of knowing, integrating the right brain (typically described as the "feminine" hemisphere, where intuition and creativity are generated) with the left brain (typically described as the "masculine" hemisphere, where logic and reason are generated). And, they challenge the pat idea that women are more "intuitive" than men, that men are more "rational" than women. The women's movement reminds us of how much more lies within our grasp as human beings, how much more creative we can be by dropping away our role restrictions and just allowing ourselves to "be." But large evolutionary jumps, such as that suggested by the women's movement, can never develop without the long, slow, day-to-day work of confronting the inequities that exist for women in the workplace, in the media and in the home.

One very successful women's network that reflects the realities of women on the job is 9to5: The National Association of Working Women, which, as a national membership organization, links women office workers into a support and advocacy network. 9to5 got its start in 1972, when a group of ten women employed in downtown Boston offices met to discuss the quality of their work experiences.

Using the name "9to5", later popularized in the Jane Fonda-Lily Tomlin-Dolly Parton film by that name, the women began to organize and to dig out the facts of life for women office workers. What they found was that over 20 million women, about 10 percent of the entire US population, are employed as office workers, with, at that time, an average salary for clerical workers of $8128 per year; and that 95 percent of all working women earn less than $10,000 annually. Using this information as their catalyst, the women in 9to5 went on to set up The National Association of Working Women, with members in fifty US states, Canada and Europe, and twenty-five chapters. 9to5 has been highly effective in drawing attention to the concerns of its constituency, having secured raises, promotions and back-pay settlements for thousands of women. More than anything else, 9to5 has identified a large, unorganized constituency, translating hunches and feelings about women's office experiences into dollars-and-cents facts around which they can organize.

9to5 was the harbinger for the rise of women's business networks that now meet in every industry at all levels of organization—helping women move up the corporate ladder, find new jobs within their companies, change careers and become board members.

Women have also created their own executive "clubs," which restrict membership to certain income levels and hierarchical rank. "The exclusive [women's] networks disturbed me at first," Carol Kleiman, author of *Women's Networks*, told *USA Today* in February 1983. "Some sound just like the old sororities. But people have the right to organize within their own groups."

For women belonging to these networks, their support value is immeasurable.

Thus the women's movement comprises many networks, working on many issues, including such concerns as creating a clearinghouse for information on marital and date rape (Women's History Research Center), establishing a women's media network (The Women's Institute for Freedom of the Press), monitoring federal actions regarding women (Women USA), working to eliminate violence against women (simply named, Women Against Violence Against Women), identifying shelters for battered women (Working on Wife Abuse), supporting displaced homemakers (Displaced Homemakers Network), and establishing networks of peer support among professional women (New England Women Business Owners), to name just a few of the hundreds of thousands of women's groups. (See *Women's Action Alliance*, edited by Jane Williamson *et al.*, and *Women's Networks*, by Carol Kleiman, for extensive listings.)

While no one of the networks is the women's movement, each is a hologram, reflecting the larger women's movement; taken as a whole, they constitute an immense metanetwork of shared perspectives, and they are moving us all toward a new understanding of what women, and men, can be.

Networking for peace

In war, almost everyone becomes powerless and subject to rule by a few. In nuclear war, absolutely everyone becomes powerless after the first explosions.

Peace movements are as old as history, waxing and waning in visibility and strength depending upon the involvements of the world's military at any moment. During the late 1960s, the peace movement (better known as the antiwar movement), had a tremendous impact on international foreign policy, and the dramatic consequences of that era still reverberate as we approach the year 2000. Vietnam provided the collective political baptism for the largest generation in history.

The image of the world at peace is beautiful—and largely unknown in our recorded history. History, as the books read, is rarely more than an accounting of one war after another, with countries and borders changing before new maps could even be drawn.

But now the stakes are higher than ever before, so high that the question can no longer be framed as a choice between war and peace. Rather, since 6 August 1945, the choice is between planetary survival and utter destruction. Despite the deeply disturbing comments of politicians who make mindless statements such as "Nuclear war is winnable," it is clear to anyone who has seriously studied the effects of nuclear war and its aftermath that no one can win a nuclear war.

With perhaps the oldest lineage in the network ecology we have studied, today's global peace movements trace their roots to 1815 when a few Quaker Peace Societies formed in the wake of the Napoleonic Wars. In his classic study *The History of Peace*, A. C. F. Beales describes five fundamental roads to peace explored by the nineteenth-century peace movement: arbitration, an international authority, international law, sanctions and disarmament. In 1930 he wrote, "I was surprised to find that every single idea current today about peace and war was being preached by organized bodies over a century ago. . . ."

More than a half century later, these five roads still comprise the greater part of the political agenda for world peace.

The aphorism "Where there's a will, there's a way" expresses the strength and weakness of these five roads. Over almost two centuries, the world community has acquired enormous experience with the *ways* of peace—developing methods and institutions of arbitration, establishing the United Nations as an international authority, progressing toward the codification and adjudication of international law and experimenting with a variety of sanctions. Disarmament, the acknowledged goal and capstone of the traditional global peace movement, has been the most elusive of these roads to peace. Missing in this noble plan has been a sufficient world constituency with a *will* to peace, the real prerequisite to disarmament.

Coincident with the first United Nations Special Session on Disarmament in 1978, the "Colloquium on the Societal Context for Disarmament" was a forum for discussing the will to peace. A recurrent theme in this conference was the need for a change in perceptions and values, the need for people and nations to "catch up" to the radically new nature of war and peace in the twentieth century. Lasting peace, the conferees felt, is only possible through the attainment of some global value consensus. This emphasis on values now is realism, not idealism—today it is idealism to think that true disarmament is possible without a preceding or an accompanying value shift.

The systems theorist Ervin Laszlo suggests four basic perceptions that need to gain influence as the foundation for peace: the "symbiosis" theory of human relationships, the "altruism is pragmatic" insight, the "unity in diversity" thesis and the "multi-level loyalty" concept.

We believe that the Invisible Planet represents evidence that a value shift with just these characteristics is underway and already widespread. Virtually all the networks of our sample reject the idea that aggression and violence are the natural basis for human relationships. Most networks positively affirm the interdependence of all people and of people with the whole planet. Networkers in our sample actively search for threads of unity while protecting the diversity of individuals, groups and cultures. Many networks explicitly state their concern with all the interdependent levels of connection, their responsibility for local and global issues alike. We place our greatest hope for the eventual achievement of global peace in the total panorama of this network.

Robert Muller (see Chapter 8) describes the "new global community values" that have emerged out of experience with "our planet's first universal organization." Muller's "four globalisms"—globalism in space, globalism in time, global institutions and global education—are paralleled by the whole-system values appearing at each level of network activity.

Globalism in space, for example, involves our new perceptions of the whole earth, externally from space and internally from planet-wide data gathering, which underlie the emerging whole-system values. Remarkably, our network research reveals a complementary "global perspective" operating at the local level. A good instance is provided by members of the *Rain* magazine collective, one of the first appropriate technology groups. They compiled *The Portland Book* as "a slice of the whole earth," a whole-system overview with attendant practical detail that perceived Portland, Oregon, USA, as a complex local system embedded in multiple layers of interdependent systems.

The appearance of global values now is accompanied by revisions of personal, local, regional and national values. Global values are inclusive, representing the integrity of all levels of human and planetary organization. Myriad clusters of people acting with a new worldview are the precursors to a sudden, species-wide value shift toward human transformation and global peace.

Predicting worldview shifts is like predicting earthquakes: we think the precursors of a shift indicate that dramatic change is sure to come, but we do not know when it will happen. Of course, whether you think worldview shifts are as real as earthquakes depends on your view of evolution.

A popular retort to current talk about weapons freezes, reduction, disarmament and the like is this: "We have always had war, and we always will have war." Disbelief that any meaningful change in the current balance of terror is possible rests on the assumption that evolutionary change happens very gradually over a very long time. Many people deny the possibility that there is ever anything truly "new under the sun"; and, consequently, they remain blind to the potential of momentous planetary change within their lifetimes.

General systems theory has convinced us that the model of emergent evolution is more likely to hold the clues to our human history than the prevailing social version of Darwinian genetic fitness. Emergent theories portray evolution as periods of sluggish continuity punctuated by sudden appearances of new entities and behaviors—evolution zigzags its way toward greater complexity, each important advance marked by crisis and uncertainty (see Chapter 10).

On the scale of even sudden evolutionary change, however, our human days and years are still slow-motion frames that make the perception of large-scale change difficult. An emergent event may require many years before the full impact of the novelty unfolds in personal/social change involving masses of people. Our optimistic assessment of the prospects for global peace is rooted in the belief that we are today witnessing the leading edge of a tidal wave of change set into motion in part by three coincident emergent events that occurred forty years ago.

Global historians of the future are likely to mark the second half of 1945 as one of the great watershed moments of human evolution. In June, the charter of the United Nations (UN) was ratified. In August of that year, nuclear weapons were used for the first time. In December, ENIAC, the first electronic computer, was declared operational.

The seed of knowledge that exploded over Hiroshima signaled the emergence of a new fact in human affairs with enormous implications for war and peace, the potential of species-wide death. As the first successful species-wide planetary organization, the United Nations is also a novelty in terrestrial history. Although the appearance of the computer was less dramatic than the other two events, we now recognize that it was equally momentous, heralding the emergence of what has come to be called the Information Age, the basis for species-wide communication.

Computers, global organization and the nuclear threat are now converging on civilization's center stage.

A network of nations

As though a cosmic compensation for our explosive entry into the Atomic Age, the process of forming a world organization was completed during the same period. While anyone who cared to look could instantly see that the shape of human destiny was irrevocably changed by nuclear weapons, the United Nations had to survive and grow before its novelty and necessity could be acknowledged. Is it in an accident of history that these two events are so entwined?

Looking at the UN through our conceptual filter of networking, we see, not surprisingly, a very complicated organization. Like most large, modern institutions, the UN is a blend of personal networks, hierarchy and bureaucracy. The UN makes use of graded ranks of authority, of specialized departments governed by policies and of innumerable personal ties inside and outside the organization. After our interview with Dr Muller (see Chapter 8), we perceived that the UN also makes use of group-network organization.

The Economic and Social Council (ECOSOC), for example, coordinates a network of relatively autonomous organizational participants who cooperate on the basis of shared values. Intergovernmental agencies and nongovernmental organizations are independent bodies with their own mandates, internal forms of organization, sources of support and constituencies. ECOSOC does not control the behavior of these member organizations but rather facilitates cooperation along lines of shared interests. Many other activities of the UN, such as the International Year programs, are also group networking examples.

When we shift our perspective to the globe as a whole, looking again at the UN through network eyes, we see an even more dramatic manifestation of large-scale networking—the network of nations coordinated through the United Nations. Sovereignty, the bane of internationalists, is the declaration of nations that they are relatively autonomous entities. Given the persistence of sovereignty as an international fact of life, the UN has not functioned in the past thirty-seven years as a "supergovernment" but rather has acquired a diplomatic persona more nearly like that of a nation.

In the networks we have studied, the coordinating group typically has a charter, an office, a staff, publications and other features very much like the participant organizations with whom it establishes peer relationships. Similarly, the United Nations does not function at some higher rung of authority than nations, but rather horizontally, dealing with nations as equals. Nations send ambassadors to other nations and to the United Nations. Bryant Wedge, an early proponent of the US National Peace Academy, found, in a study of UN Secretariat personnel, that many members tend to develop a nationalistic attitude about the UN itself, evincing great concern for the survival of the institution. This seems natural to us.

The world organization we seek may not lie in the institution of the United Nations *per se*, but rather in the larger network of nations of which the UN is a part. Viewed in this light, the UN has not somehow "failed" to achieve supernational status against the obstructions of national sovereignty but rather has successfully established its status as a "world power" while simultaneously catalyzing the still-forming metanetwork of nations. A network of relatively sovereign nations cohering through shared values and interests is quite possibly more achievable and healthy for humanity than the creation of a supernational coercive authority.

Peacing

One of the sixty-four hexagrams that comprise the Chinese *Book of Changes* (*I Ching*) is "T'ai." In English, this hexagram is called "Peace." Richard Wilhelm writes, "T'ai is a difficult word to translate. It means contentment, rest, peace, in the positive sense of unobstructed, completed union, bringing about a time of flowering and greatness."

Imagine, for a moment, what a society expressing unobstructed, complete union, reflected in a time of flowering and greatness, could mean. Peace is a condition of realizing human potential in its fullest sense. Peace is a value that many people hold as good. War, with which it is usually contrasted, is a value that many people hold as bad. In the *I Ching*, "Peace" is contrasted with "Standstill." "*Standstill* and *Peace* stand in natural opposition to each other," the commentary reads.

Over the years, peace has been defined in two ways: negatively, as the absence of war, a passive state of no violent conflict, and positively, as the precondition for the full release of the cornucopia of human potentials. Many sources are generating a global *will* to peace.

Positive and negative are complements, each an aspect of the other. Today's world nuclear movement is extraordinarily diverse but united on the shared negative perception of peace as the absence of nuclear war. The power of the movement lies in its ability to represent a universal threat to survival without requiring agreement on any other beliefs. This aspect of global peace networks will ebb and flow according to changing conditions, but the larger dynamic of evolutionary transition will continue to increase the broader constituency for human transformation and positive global peace.

We say "to war" but not "to peace." There is no verb for peace.

We make peace, talk peace and at moments live peacefully; but there is no action word *peace*. If there were, the networks that we have identified under the banner of the Invisible Planet would be *peacing*, using the word as naturally as they do healing or sharing or evolving. What the networks do say is that they are networking, which means being part of the process of global peace.

CHAPTER 6

Inner networking

In a vivid portrayal of the meaning of a personal search, one dancer in the Boston contact improvisation group called River darts from point to point, frantically asking which way to go, raving her need for external direction until she reaches a guide who says simply, "Go inside." The dancer folds down upon herself and that section of the dance is over.

Searching

Go inside. It is a message that has been received by millions of people in the late twentieth century.

Inner growth, personal change, evolution, transformation. Coming to grips with yourself, changing, growing. Running, practicing yoga and t'ai chi, meditating, sitting, chanting. Consulting astrology, numerology, and the *I Ching*. Reading the Seth material, and the Don Juan books. Alan Watts and Ram Dass. Therapy: rolfing, psychodrama, Gestalt, psychosynthesis, bioenergetics, T-groups. A weekend workshop.

What psychologist Abraham Maslow simply called our "human potential" became the name tag for a movement without precedent in recent human history.

Something dramatic and unpredicted spilled out of the social upheavals of the 1960s. The quest for collective social change merged with the yearning for individual personal change.

While many critics regard this transition as a leap toward narcissism, self-absorption, and delusion (including journalists such as Tom Wolfe, who wrote the quintessential article with that theme, "The Me Decade and the Third Great Awakening," in an August 1976 issue of *New York* magazine), others, particularly those who took the leap themselves, find that the difference between collective social work and individual personal work is illusory. If we truly do want to create a different society, one based on humane, equitable, loving principles, we have to also explore, alter, and reconfigure that part of the planet that we at once know best and least: ourselves.

So it was that, in the past several decades in the US and more recently in Europe, Asia and even in Soviet bloc countries, many became personal seekers and spiritual aspirants, embarked on a search for meaning. Even the born-again millions reflect this same impulse.

Whereas, once, the dominant intellectual perception was that if one really faced "true reality" one would see how awful things really are, a lighter, more optimistic outlook came to those who were willing to put pessimism aside. If we know from our own experience that we can mature beyond jealousy, allow hurts to dissipate, and convert anger into constructive action, then we can believe the same to be true of others.

This subtle but profound shift away from existential ennui, the dominant philosophical stance of the past several decades, and from the loneliness that had paralyzed so many in the twentieth century, was reflected in how people spent their time. Weekends at resorts were traded for weekends at retreats. Evening seminars replaced going to the movies. Individual alienation gave way to a sense of belonging. Words like meditation soon became modified by even more obscure terms such as transcendental, and practices like TM (Transcendental Meditation) became spiritual-fulfillment fast-food.

Many apparently new ideas were mixed with very old disciplines, as people sampled from a plentiful menu. Emphases changed: t'ai chi and yoga replaced weight-lifting and sit-ups; the "health food" movement put the concept of dieting in new perspective. Theories abounded, some complementary, some contradictory: our emotions, many said, are locked in our muscles, others said between our muscles, while still others said in our organs, while yet others said not in our bodies at all but, rather, in our minds, which merely reflect the sad state of our bodies. Meditate with a mantra (a special word or sound), meditate without a mantra. Watch the breath, hold the breath, breathe in, breathe out. Relax the back, hold the spine straight. Imagine a brilliant light in your mind, empty your mind of thought.

Out of this *mélange* of insights, theories, and conjectures arose centers and movements and disciplines too numerous to count, too varied to categorize, yet too meaningful to their participants to be ignored. Certainly there was much to criticize and even more to caricature in the fledgling attempts at ceremonializing and systematizing the process of self-understanding, and egregious mistakes were made—some by fools, others by well-intentioned if over-zealous seekers—yet the basic message of the greater movement reflected the age-old quest of inner fulfillment as a complement to, not a contradiction of, earthly peace.

Still, the field was littered with charlatans and exploiters, some simply hungry for the buck, others twisted and demented, preying on the naïveté of the people around them—the most pitiful, ghastly example being the Reverend Jim Jones in Guyana. It was easy to fixate on the dishonorable elements—which is largely what the media chose to do, sometimes pinpointing and exposing the snake-oil hawkers, but all too often lumping everything together.

Just as is the case with physical objects—some are beautiful and of rare quality, while others are shoddy and useless—so it is with methods and disciplines: the personal- and spiritual-growth worlds are populated by the elegant and the authentic, as well as by the spurious, shabbily produced imitations. To grow within, we must be discriminating about the nourishment we choose to ingest. As the sages have told us, there is no neutral ground in the universe—either we contribute or we detract. It's as simple as that.

There is no single right plan for personal growth, nor is there a central synod for the new spirituality. This chapter points to some of the connecting points for these unique networks—unique because to pursue and nurture and accept these personal and spiritual practices is surely a very important way of manifesting love in the world.

Personal growth

It is difficult to separate the personal-growth (or human potential or consciousness) movement from the many influences that have created a revival of interest in spiritual practice. The human potential movement arose in part due to the writings of one classically trained psychologist, Abraham Maslow. Rather than looking at neurotic people and their problems, Maslow chose to study creative people and their possibilities. Maslow's 1962 book *Toward a Psychology of Being* popularized the concept of *self-actualization*, the process by which people motivate themselves to grow, evolve, and become more creative. Within his model, Maslow pinpointed the transformative moments that people live through—those *peak experiences* that metamorphose people's lives, making them more than they were before, propelling them toward the "farthest reaches of being human" (the title of one of his books, posthumously published).

Buttressed by the writings of Carl Rogers, Rollo May and Fritz Perls, just to name a few, humanistic psychology made a fragile claim to a place on the academic map, formed its own professional organization, the Association for Humanistic Psychology, began publication of a scholarly journal, *The Journal of Humanistic Psychology*, and over the next two decades served as one of the primary hatcheries for scores of new psychotherapeutic methods.

With this miscellany of instruments for coping with personal dilemmas, we can become fluent in the language of our bodies, observe our birth experiences creeping into our behaviour at the dinner table, train our minds to reduce blood pressure, mobilize our immune systems to reverse life-threatening illnesses, and design more beautiful mental images of ourselves that will soon show on our faces, in our limbs, and in our lives, allowing us to work more effortlessly, run more lightly, sleep more soundly. There is a technology for every small hamlet nestled in our psyches: some are expensive and known to millions; others, virtually unknown, are passed along without cost in moments of crisis—like the person who teaches a friend the principles of progressive relaxation in the midst of an anxious long-distance telephone call.

Countless networks have emanated from the cornucopia of techniques, many of them derived from ancient teachings. Popularized, offered not only to initiates but to lay people as well, the techniques are really new again. With thousands, perhaps millions of people practicing them, a new form of awareness is in the process of being born.

The human potential movement is inseparably yoked to the establishment of meeting places, called centers, that were started in the 1960s and 1970s. Oldest and most famous of these is Esalen, a "center" that has no direct connection to any of the others yet by its very existence has served as a symbolic template. Unpretentiously snuggled into a cliff beneath Highway 1 on the spectacular continental edge of the Pacific, steamed by hot springs once frequented by the Esselen Indians, Esalen has both natural beauty as a distinction as well as the history of being the original "growth" center in the United States.

Esalen came about because of Michael Murphy, a native of Bolina, California. Murphy, now an accomplished author, a serious long-distance runner and a "citizen diplomat," got the idea to establish a center to explore his consuming interest in philosophy and religion, particularly Eastern religion. After graduating from Stanford, Murphy became one of the first 1960s seekers to travel to India (where he stayed for some time at the Sri Aurobindo Ashram in Pondicherry). Returning with no clear plan for his life, Murphy suggested to his grandmother that he might take over family property at the hot springs in Big Sur, and before long, Murphy and a few friends had opened an "institute."

Although it was originally conceived with a more intellectual orientation, Esalen soon became known as a place where people would go for "experiences" (now a very common word, like "relationships", both of which have collected a family of semantic innuendoes that they simply did not have before the 1960s). Eminent and sometimes bizarre luminaries rising on the new psychological frontier came to deliver week-long and even month-long sessions, and people spent extraordinary amounts of money to listen to, take part in, and evaluate the presentations. All kinds of new techniques—from pummeling apart the connective tissue between the muscles (innocuously called rolfing, after its developer, Ida Rolf) to elaborating new models of the universe—were thrashed out in the Esalen bungalows. As time went on the personal orientation of the seminars expanded to embrace social and scientific issues, and as its contribution to the "citizen diplomacy" movement, Esalen was sponsoring its own Soviet-American exchange program.

While growth centers have at times functioned as the staging ground for absurd and sometimes destructive ideas, these new centers for a new kind of learning have also served a powerful purpose in authenticating the value of inner knowledge, corroborating the magnitude of affective (emotional) learning. Further, the human potential movement has proffered permissions that depart from the cultural norm: for men to cry, for women to be angry, for people to confront the dark underbelly of existence, to wrestle with it, and to ingest it, composting pain into wisdom and experience. The panic that comes with loss, the wounds of rejection, the terror of dying, the awesome fear of giving birth are the daily agendas of growth sessions.

The workshops and lectures are merely one aspect of this imprecise realm known as personal growth. One may start with a "training," a jargonistic way of describing concentrated short courses, in which a particular way of looking at the world is espoused. While some "trainees" then become proselytes of that particular approach, volunteering or perhaps being paid to work for the organization, most people then move on to something else, perhaps to another training (yes, dilettantes appear here, too) or perhaps more selectively to learning about diet or exercise or meditation. A massage (or polarity or shiatsu or some other physical treatment or bodily reeducation such as Alexander method or Feldenkrais technique) may come next, possibly coincident with studying yoga or t'ai chi or aikido or inaugurating a daily exercise.

While there is no formal relationship between any two points in the network, an offhand remark or flyer on a desk or direct suggestion may guide someone from Point A to Point B. For example, two students in an Iyengar yoga group strike up a conversation after class, one mentions a dream, the other responds with an anecdote about a workshop she attended the weekend before, and within a few moments, the person who had the dream has decided to attend the Intensive Journal Workshop the next time it is offered. There is no explicit connection between B. K. S. Iyengar (who developed the yoga system) and Ira Progoff (who developed the Intensive Journal Method), yet their disciplines both are familiar stopping points on people's journeys inward. In a very large view, there is a *Gestalt* alliance among all the byways concerned with personal development, a coherence that ultimately links all the areas of networking addressed in this book. Anthropologist Virginia Hine puts it this way in her paper "How do we get from here to there? The conceptual paradigm shift."

Many a down to earth anti-nuke farmer, for example, has a beloved and therefore influential son or daughter involved in

Zen. A worker in a local rent-control project of the consumer movement is also a follower of a Swami presiding over an international network of meditation centers. An est graduate lives in a commune that is tied into the holistic health movement and is currently serving as technical advisor to an ad hoc corporate task force. A teacher in an alternative school practices Silva Mind Control and devotes her spare time to fighting multinational corporations selling non-nutritious baby foods in Brazil.

Here we see the personal and the social in a productive interplay, enhancing one's ability to be active in the world. But the bias against self-exploration is deeply ingrained in our Western culture. (Try consulting a thesaurus for synonyms for words like self-exploration and prepare yourself for a deluge of unflattering terms, including: self-centered, self-important, self-seeking, and self-absorbed, as well as conceited, egotistical and smug.)

The journey within is very long indeed, frequently leading people to a new philosophical view, one that may stand alongside, absorb, or possibly replace one's religious beliefs. A concern with self coexists with a concern for the context within which the self exists, that vast amorphous unknown quantity (or is it quality?) called Universe. This is the point of departure for the spiritual growth networks whose numbers have mushroomed in the past twenty years.

Spiritual growth

What is spiritual growth and why do people become involved, indeed engrossed, in it? Spiritual growth makes people happier and provides a framework for understanding the biggest questions of all: What is the nature of the universe? and Who is this "I" that asks this question?

The development of the spiritual growth movement was helped by at least three apparently unrelated phenomena rooted in the 1960s: the space program, which gave us physical proof that our pearly blue planet spins in a sea that is mostly empty (mirroring both the reality being revealed beneath the lens of the powerful electron microscope and ancient Eastern cosmological wisdom, which speaks of "the void" and "the Absolute" as the same thing);

the widespread availability of psychotropic (mind-altering) drugs such as marijuana, LSD, mescaline and psilocybin, which reportedly enabled their users to briefly experience states of universal "oneness" that had long been described by religious seers and mystics; and jet travel and electronic communication, which greased the tracks for cross-cultural connections. Science, technology, and the market place made it easy to accept and have access to what theologian Harvey Cox has called the "turning east," one more stitch in the global community quilt.

The connection between Eastern teachings and Western followings did not begin when the Beatles went to India to meet Maharishi Mahesh Yogi—the incident that many regard as the catalytic moment in the life of the new spirituality. The tradition of Indian masters, in particular, coming to the West can be traced to the late nineteenth century, when the British established dominance in India. In the US, the history of the arrival of Eastern religion can be traced to one seminal event caused by one remarkable individual: Swami Vivekananda, a 30-year-old classically trained Vedantic monk, a student of the Indian sage Ramakrishna, who traveled at his own initiative to the Parliament of World Religions at the 1893 Chicago World's Fair. Vivekananda, then unknown to both the other speakers and the audience, is reported to have given an electrifying speech. His reputation spread quickly, and he decided to stay in the United States, where he was invited to travel from place to place, largely at the invitation of the unconventional intellectual/Bohemian community then in the making. During his time in the United States, he created the Ramakrishna Vedanta Society, which still exists today. (Vivekananda's visits to Boston, where he was particularly well received, were partially responsible for New England bluebloods being nicknamed "Boston Brahmins.")

In 1920, Paramahansa Yogananda came to the United States, helping to bring the practice of yoga to the West. Through Yogananda's organization, the Self-Realization Fellowship, some traditional Vedantic teachings (dating as far back as perhaps 4000 BC) were disseminated in the West through correspondence courses as well as meetings.

Over the next several decades, other classically trained Indian spiritual figures came to the United States, spreading knowledge previously locked in the East, and they attracted considerable followings. Among these people have been four important and very different figures who began their journeys in India.

Meher Baba, known to his followers as the Avatar (meaning the incarnation of God), lived most of his adult life in silence, and made two visits to the United States before his death in 1969. A quote from Meher Baba, "Don't worry, be happy," became something of a slogan in the 1960s, serving as a common point of reference for his following which neither proselytized nor actively sought converts.

Hazarat Inayat Khan was the vehicle for the Westernization of Sufism, a word thought to be derived from the Greek *sophia* (wisdom), a variegated tradition based on teachings originating in Hinduism, Buddhism, Zoroastrianism, the mystery schools of ancient Egypt and Greece, and Islam. Headed today by his son Pir Vilayat Khan, the Sufi order is a nondogmatic path that recognizes the common heritage of all religious traditions.

Krishnamurti, who ultimately broke ranks with the British Theosophists (who had identified him as the messiah while he was still a young boy in India), eventually established bases in California and Switzerland, where he gave talks until his death in February, 1986. Krishnamurti's basic message of spiritual self-reliance is a pertinent complement to networking theory.

Maharishi Mahesh Yogi, perhaps the most visible of these teachers, has brought transcendental meditation to the West. Although the TM program separates itself from any overt spiritual connections (choosing instead the somewhat sanitized subtitle "the science of creative intelligence"), Maharishi is a Vedic scholar who has undertaken the task of translating many scriptures still locked in Sanskrit. TM reached its peak of public visibility in the mid-1970s, when Maharishi appeared on the "Merv Griffin" television show, resurfacing again a few years later, when the press began to report on the TM Siddhis (literally meaning "perfection") program, an expensive and extensive training program in which meditators reportedly learn to bring the mind and body into a state of coherence and thus levitate.

The movement has also included American teachers schooled in Buddhist practice. Rick Fields, himself a student of Buddhism and documenter of what he has identified as American Buddhism, describes the phenomenon this way in *The Next Whole Earth Catalog*:

It has taken about 2500 years for Buddhism to reach America. Thoreau . . . translated and published possibly the first mahayana sutra [scripture] in America (from the French in *The Dial*, 1854) and . . . realized what the Orientals mean by contemplation as he sat in his sunny doorway one morning at Walden. . . . D. T. Suzuki, the first patriarch of American Zen, took an editing and translating job in La Salle, Illinois in 1897, and there have been Zen Buddhists of some sort here ever since. In the sixties, formal Zen practice became generally available, and in the seventies Americans trained in the forest monasteries of Southeast Asia returned home, while Tibetan exiles, having crossed the Himalayas on foot, arrived by jet.

[There are] three traditional subdevelopments of Buddhist development . . . the Theravadin school is the earliest . . . and now survives chiefly in Burma, Thailand, and Ceylon. Mahayana, a later development, based on the idea of the Bodhisattva, who postpones entry into Nirvana in order to work with others, is found in China, Japan, Korea, and Vietnam. Vajrayana, or Tantric Buddhism, developed in northern India [and] was practiced in Tibet, Mongolia, and Sikkim.

The now considerable network of Zen (Mahayana) Buddhist centers—from the famous Zen Center of San Francisco started by Shunruyu Suzuki Roshi (author of *Zen Mind, Beginner's Mind*), to the Zen Center in Rochester, New York, started by Roshi Philip Kapleau (author of *The Three Pillars of Zen*)—have reached many North Americans. Teachers coming out of Tibet, such as Chogyam Trungpa, Rinpoche, who founded the Naropa Institute, in Boulder, Colorado, have extended the Vajrayana tradition to the West. Americans Joseph Goldstein (who stumbled upon Buddhism while in the Peace Corps in Asia) and Jack Kornfield, among others, have imported the Theravadin tradition to the US, now based at the Insight Meditation Center, in Barre, Massachusetts—formerly a Catholic monastery.

Among the most impressive people to come to the West in recent years is Tenzin Gyatso, His Holiness, the 14th Dalai Lama of Tibet. The Dalai Lama is the exiled spiritual and political leader of Tibet, a country occupied since 1959 by the Chinese. Recognized at the age of 2 as the "incarnation" of the previous (13th) Dalai

Lama, he was subsequently given an intense course of study in Buddhist scripture and logic. The Dalai Lama is symbolic as a transitional figure between East and West, one who deals both with the personal and the social, the spiritual and the political realities of daily life.

Speaking at Harvard Divinity School in February 1981 on the nature of the guru-disciple relationship, Pascal Kaplan, who wrote his doctoral dissertation on this topic, drew the following distinction between cults, which he believes appeal to people's egos, and authentic spiritual practice, which he regards as aiding the dissolution of the ego, a step aspired to on many paths:

> A cult figure will orient his or her teaching and organization to the process of enhancing the ego life of those who come under that person's influence rather than enhancing the spiritual processes. Cults are very precise in defining membership—who's in and who's out. Whoever's in is good, right, and holy. Whoever's out is everything else. In cults, the emphasis is on hierarchy—*my* place and *my* role—with merit badges and Boy Scout ranks and knowing one's place and having one's role clearly defined.

In the many spiritual networks, such distinctions as "who's in" and "who's out" are not only inappropriate but at cross-purposes with the desires of the aspirants. For every spiritual group *member*, there are dozens more people who participate autonomously in many spiritual disciplines, creating the links and thus the greater network of affiliated spiritual teachings. Even so, many people have been sucked into personality cults from which extrication is difficult. This does not mean that any of these groups or methods is "bad" as such. It does mean, however, that leaving a close-knit community, particularly one based on shared spiritual bonds, is very difficult.

Just as the East has spawned its own school of what has been called "freshwater spiritualism," so has the West. The new reformism in Christianity has been reported in the process primarily as the turn toward fundamentalism. Yet there is another strand with a typically Christian message, one that acknowledges a many-dimensional reality within which Jesus Christ is one, albeit central, figure. *The Course in Miracles*, two volumes reportedly dictated to an agnostic woman, then an assistant professor of medical psychology at Columbia University, from a "higher source", has been one of the documents for the transmission of this third force in Christianity. "Miracle" groups have sprung up in many places, with people taking the course (which offers a program of study for every one of 365 days) and meeting to discuss their studies. While many aspects of traditional Christianity come through the pages of *The Course in Miracles*, it is reminiscent of the Christian mystics and carries a message that encourages the use of affirmations (repetitions of positive thoughts) and visualizations (creating mental pictures). Although less formalized and without a central written doctrine, a parallel practice is evolving out of classical Judaism. In Philadelphia and Boston, B'nai Or, started by Reb Zalman Schachter Shalomi, are Jewish Congregations that combine both traditional and alternative methods of worship. The entire congregation participates in meditation, storytelling, singing, dancing, and sharing of prayers.

Any thorough discussion of the "consciousness movement" must acknowledge the considerable upsurge of interest in the psychic and the occult in the past several decades, tantalizing and potentially absorbing practices that are often confused with spiritual traditions. It is often the case that when people meditate, or engage in some other spiritual practice in a disciplined way, they report that extrasensory faculties become more finely honed, enabling them to see beyond the five senses, demonstrating clairvoyance (the ability to perceive things that are out of visible range), clairaudience (the ability to hear beyond the immediate audio range), and other remarkable feats. (For some people, these "powers" appear to be innate.)

Westerners, long divorced from nonmaterial perceptions, are fascinated by such "impossible" abilities. However, ancient teachers and modern masters are adamant in stating that advanced "powers" are not the point, or the goal, or even a desirable objective of spiritual practice—they are merely its occasional byproduct. Is "seeing" an aura, described as colored halo around the body, any different from being able to see the skin on people's faces? For every layer of reality we unfold, there is another and another and another. Seeing auras or having preknowledge of an event, or being able to hear across great distances, or being able to bend physical objects with the mind do not *make* people spiritual.

Much of the life of the spiritual growth networks blossoms

because people read books like Itzhak Bentov's *Stalking the Wild Pendulum: On the Mechanics of Consciousness* and recognize experiences that they have not seen confirmed elsewhere, or because people see the sculpture and hear the poetry of Mirtala in her exquisite film *The Human Journey*, or because people pass along pamphlets such as *Conversations with John*, edited by David Spangler (author of *Revelation: The Birth of A New Age*, cofounder of the Lorian Association, a spiritually-oriented group, and one of the early members of Findhorn, the spiritual community situated in Scotland), or *Steps Toward Inner Peace* by Peace Pilgrim, the woman who walked across America for twenty-eight years "practicing peace."

While spiritual practice sits at the core of many people's lives, for others the very idea of a spiritual dimension in life seems atavistic, primitive, unenlightened. This perspective is shared by many intellectuals as well as by such groups as the American Humanist Association, who deplore talk of "other realities," imploring instead that people take full charge of their own powers and not abdicate responsibility to an unseen "greater force." There is a very loving and enriching quality to the Humanist message, one that satisfies many of the same yearnings that impel people toward spiritual practice.

Yet another dimension to the idea of spiritual growth is being explored from a feminist perspective. The work of nineteenth century historians such as Bachofen documents a distinct heritage of humans worshiping a female, rather than a male, deity.

In the twentieth century, the scholar Erich Neumann continued this research, which is documented in his extensive work *The Great Mother*. The physician S. Esther Harding followed with *Woman's Mysteries*. (Both Neumann and Harding were students of C. G. Jung.) Interest in this work was revived in the late 1960s with the publication of Elizabeth Gould Davis's widely read book, *The First Sex*, and by the end of the 1970s with the writings of theologian Mary Daly (*Beyond God the Father*), Anne Kent Rush's exquisitely designed and easy to read *Moon, Moon*, and art historian Merlin Stone's more scholarly works *When God Was a Woman* and *Ancient Mirrors of Womanhood*. Together, these works represent a new interpretation of religious history, one that encompasses the later patriarchal traditions that have inspired even the most modern of spiritual networks. People gather for festivals connected with the moon, the spring and fall equinoxes, the summer and winter solstices, to honor these ancient traditions.

Carol P. Christ (yes, that's her real name), a theological scholar, forecasts the impact of this new trend in spirituality in her book *Diving Deep and Surfacing: Women Writers on Spiritual Quest*:

> Recently women have begun to write about the connections between spirituality and personal and spiritual change. They have pointed out that women's spiritual quest provides new visions of individual and shared power that can inspire a transformation of culture and society. . . . Women's spiritual quest is thus not an alternative to women's social quest, but rather is one dimension of the larger quest women have embarked upon to create a new world.

Ultimately, the purpose of spiritual development is to enrich daily life. By translating sometimes abstract and abstruse teachings into ordinary situations, we make spiritual development a real, concrete contribution to the everyday world.

One working spiritual network

One special network that appears to bridge the esoteric realms and the gut reality of everyday existence has emerged from the transformation of Ram Dass—in his previous life a psychologist at Harvard, named Richard Alpert, who catapulted to fame alongside Timothy Leary. Ram Dass was one of the first psychedelic experimenters to observe the ephemeral nature of "getting high." By the end of the 1960s, he had sloughed off his previous identity in favor of a spiritual path, which he pursued to India, where he became a student of the spiritual master Neem Karoli Baba. Returning to an enthusiastic American reception, Ram Dass went on the first of many lecture tours during which he spoke humorously of his experiences with spiritual development. He convened gatherings, some of which took place at his family homestead on Webster Lake, in Franklin, New Hampshire, where interested people camped out for several days to meditate, chant and listen to him speak.

Although people tried to become his disciples, Ram Dass did not accept the role of guru to a devoted following, and beyond that, his ability to poke fun at himself has kept him in touch with his own humanity. That quality, coupled with some embarrassing mistakes and rather substantial errors of judgment that he was willing to make public (in such classic essays as "Egg on my beard"), have endeared the man to many who would otherwise have written him off.

What fewer people know is that Ram Dass, and his network of friends who first met as students of Neem Karoli Baba in India, have created what amounts to a Spiritual Good Works Factory. In the mid-1970s, he established the Hanuman (after the Indian God-monkey by that name) Foundation as a nonprofit tax-exempt corporation to which he donated his earnings from his lectures and his books (notably *Be Here Now, The Only Dance There Is*, and *Grist for the Mill*, which he coauthored with Stephen Levine).

"An institution grows through expanding and contracting," Ram Dass explains in a 1985 telephone interview from his parents' home near Boston. "The Hanuman Foundation accordion is pulled in right now."

For a decade, the Hanuman Foundation has comprised three separate, independent projects: the Prison-Ashram Project, the Dying Project, and the Hanuman Foundation Tape Library. While the Tape Library continues to sell audiotapes of the Hanuman network's lectures, the Dying Project, started by Stephen Levine to help terminally ill people to practice "conscious dying," and carried on by Dale Borglum, is in a "holding pattern" until it relocates from its original base in New Mexico to a more urban setting.

Meanwhile, the Prison-Ashram Project has completed *We're All Doing Time*, its final volume of a three-book series. Run for over a decade by Bo and Sita Lozoff, the Prison-Ashram Project:

> ... provides information and encouragement to prisoners who would like to use their time for spiritual training. As well as introducing them to meditation, yoga, and spiritual ideas (not religious), we also try to help people avoid getting caught or seduced into various traps or trips that often go along with these studies. Our emphasis is on a light, good-humored, non-preachy perspective.
>
> We've been fortunate through the years to gain solid credibility with the American correctional establishment. These linkages have taught us a great deal about relating to

the culture at large, since we have usually considered
ourselves to be far outside that culture. It's nice to see how
service tends to assimilate us into the mainstream and break
down illusory walls which were our own creations in the first
place.

When the originators first envisioned the Prison-Ashram Project,
they expected that their constituency would be drawn largely from
counterculture types who had been imprisoned for drug or political
offenses. Much to their surprise, however, they found instead that
"most of the thousands of prisoners who wrote to us were 35 to
45 years old and had been in prison up to 25 years already. Or
they were people who had been sentenced to 200 years plus life;
people who had less than an eighth grade education."

The response moved Lozoff to reexamine his original assumptions and to rethink how to present yoga and meditation within
the prison walls. As a result, he developed what he calls "prison
yoga. . . . We can help people convert their prison experience into
a monastic one," he told *Sufi Times*, "but it's a very particular
monastic environment—one lived within an atmosphere of
hostility, hatred, and suspicion."

If one branch of the tree whose roots can be traced to Neem
Karoli Baba is shedding its leaves, another is sprouting them. In
1985, Ram Dass became chair of the Seva (literally, service in
Sanskrit) Foundation, the international public health charity based
in Michigan. Founded in 1978 by Girija Brilliant, who holds a PhD
in public health administration, and her husband Larry Brilliant, a
medical doctor and epidemiologist, Seva has been involved
primarily in blindness prevention in Nepal and India.

Both Brilliants were instrumental in the World Health Organization smallpox eradication program in India.

In 1983 Larry Brilliant, convinced of the utility of computer
conferencing (see Chapter 7) to the medical community, founded
Network Technologies International, Inc. (NETI), a publicly traded
corporation that now markets software for "electronic meetings"
to the Fortune 1000 companies, the legal community and the
medical field.

One of NETI's earliest users was the Seva Foundation, which
may have one of the first globally distributed nonprofit boards of
directors to meet regularly "online."

"I spend about two hours a day online," Ram Dass explains. "That's how I keep up with my communication. It's amazing how much business we can do via computer."

Conscious dying? Prison yoga? Board meetings online? Contradictions in terms? No, partners in the cosmic dance.

CHAPTER 7

Networking with computers

"Computers" and "networks" are words that go well together. Perhaps too well, if you are doing a keyword search for information on people networks and don't want to wade through a lot of hardware stories.

These hardware stories, however, often contain the holon (whole-part) essence of a network. Adapting our definition of social networks: a computer network is a set of stand-alone computers cohering through shared protocols. One excellent definition of a "local-area network" appeared in the January 1983 cover story of *Personal Computing*, by David James:

> [A network] is a multiple-user, multiple-function computer system of equal units. The key here is not the multiuser configuration; indeed, a true network is less a "system" than a collection of equals. . . . In a true local-area network, roles are shared. . . . The key is that any computer in the network, regardless of where it is geographically, can access all the elements of the network—whether it's another computer, a memory-storage unit, or a printer. "Equality and fraternity" are the bywords here.

In computer networks, as in people networks, we see two patterns: *parts*—people, groups, computers, or peripherals—that have independent functions and capabilities; and a *whole* that emerges from the communication between parts, the entity of relationships called "a network."

For people networks, computers are a tool that may be used to greatly enhance the ability of individuals and small groups to act as very capable and independent node-parts in business, issue-oriented, professional, or other sorts of social networks. Computers can also be effective helpmates to the people facilitating a network, assisting in collecting, maintaining, and distributing the information that is often the "whole body" of a network.

None of the many cover stories we've seen on "computer networking" even hints at the complementary social phenomenon of "people networking" that comes bundled with every multiple-computer setup.

Social networks are organizational "media with a message." So are computer networks. If a tightly controlled company sets up a true local-area network but maintains its existing hierarchical management chart, the social and technological messages are sure to conflict. Desktop access to large databases and communications systems together with local power to prepare, process, and use information bring both independence and decision-making capability. If the social whole can't adjust to its technologically more independent parts, then trouble lies ahead.

Conversely, an organization looking to democratize its structure, distribute its decision making, and encourage creativity can use computer networks to support those social goals.

On a very personal level, we have been using computers in our work continuously since 1970 and in our home since 1978. They are part of our mental equipment now, an integral part of how our skills and thinking come together into real-world products. For us, computers enhance our humanness, doing for mental drudgery what machines did for muscle drudgery.

And, we are only at the beginning. More precisely, we are in the middle of the beginning, in a very turbulent transition time of ideas, technologies, social organization and personal consciousness. Old and new coexist right now.

Today's computer is still tied to yesterday's logic. It carries its own genetic constraint—like the external skeleton that kept the insect's brain from developing. The computer limit might be called "the von Neumann bottle-neck," the one-step-at-a-time central processing unit that controls the whole system through its linear logic. While the design strategy has been to widen the control channel from eight bits to sixteen bits, the thirty-two bit Apple Macintosh already heralds the evolutionary end of this pathway.

Future "computers" will be more like brains: they will be organized as networks. There will be no "central" processor, as there is no "chief cell" that directs the brain, no one place that controls the "whole me." Each cell is an individual, with features of biological independence, yet specialized within the neurological whole—like chips on a motherboard.

Faint hints of the network-processing strategy are seen in computers with parallel processors, or coprocessors, or the use of special processors to handle screen functions or high-precision mathematics. Broadening this perspective, local-area networks may be seen as large-scale breadboard experiments in linking functionally independent processors into one system. Stepping farther out, global computer-communications networks presage the hardware of a global brain.

Electronic networking

Electronic networking and computer conferencing are names for a remarkable new communications medium created by the merger of computer and telecommunications technologies. In contrast to computer-assisted instruction (CAI) or a conventional information utility, where people are meant to interact directly with a computer, computer-mediated communications enhances people's ability to connect with other people.

In developing our research on *people* networking, we have been assisted by *electronic* networking tools. Our personal computers and telecommunication extensions have been irreplaceable aids in dealing with the complexity of our myriad contacts and information sources.

It is our conviction that people and computer networking are developing as complementary aspects of the same evolutionary trends. While it is quite possible that computer networking will remain an elite activity, the downward plunging prices and upward leaping performance of computer power leave as an open issue the ultimate accessibility of this resource by the world's people.

As a many-to-many interactive medium, electronic networking involves: (1) a host computer and software; (2) the telephone system and its extensions; and (3) users with personal computers or terminals. Users connect through the phone system to call the host computer, enter a common "space" (literally memory space), and have access to services such as electronic mail, online conferences, electronic meetings, electronic publications, and online education.

The electronic networking *business* is concentrated in the host part of the host-phone-user system. A regional host typically consists of a minicomputer, the appropriate communications gear, sophisticated conferencing/electronic-mail software, and administrative support for the 1,000–100,000 users involved in such a network.

As a "new" medium, electronic networking combines aspects of other media in novel ways, and adds a few twists. This interactive medium provides a way for people and groups to exchange information and ideas. It is like the mail system, telephone, and face-to-face meetings in this regard.

Like the telephone, electronic networking is inherently nongeographic, precisely because the telephone acts as the point-to-point loop between one user, the host, and all other users. Meetings, by contrast, are very geographic.

With both meetings and the telephone, people communicate in real time (synchronous). Computer conferencing can likewise be synchronous, but it can also be, like the mail, at different times (asynchronous), which means you can pick up mail and respond to comments in conferences at your own convenience.

Like the phone and mail, electronic communications provides a very personal one-to-one medium. Like meetings, electronic networking offers very public spaces for small seminars, large conferences, or multifaceted information cultures. Electronic interaction may be recorded in hard copy, like mail, or experienced in ephemeral soft copy as telephone and meeting exchanges are.

While like them, electronic networking is also utterly unlike mail, phone, and in-person meetings. Because everything flows from people, through computers, to people, electronic networking interaction is preserved, that is, memorized. All communication is stored in the host computer and can be retrieved, organized, misused and transformed with all the flexibility computers allow.

As the historical record accumulates on any host computer, nongeographic communities tend to develop. People networks flower in the soil of electronic networks.

Cultures are better experienced than explained. Through messages, comments, notes, memos and other formats, people inform, question and touch one another. While obviously carrying rational content, this medium also transmits emotional color and drama. Much is said between lines.

Electronic networking is most successful when it is combined with periodic face-to-face meetings. Where in-person meetings enrich online exchanges, computer conferencing provides the continuity and contact that meetings cannot. Face-to-face and computer conferencing are complements—the ultimate combination of "high tech" and "high touch," to use John Naisbitt's term from his book *Megatrends*.

Electronic networking has been predominately a national medium, dominated in the US by large commercial systems, such as CompuServe and The Source. Because of the distance separating users of national systems, only a small portion of the online experiments have involved any offline contact.

Regional conferencing potentially provides the best balance in addressing the "distance dilemma." The benefits of electronic networking increase in value the farther apart people are as the medium helps "close the gap," while in-person meetings are easier the closer people are. In a region, such as New England, an ongoing need for contact over a wide area can be accommodated with computer conferencing and combined with the relative ease of meeting in person. Conferencing for a geographically distributed company or institution would be a similarly appropriate context for balance between in-person meetings and online contact. Many companies already successfully use electronic mail, and others, such as Digital Equipment Corporation, use computer conferencing for planning purposes within and between departments, across New England, and around the globe.

The New England Commons, a regional conferencing system based in Boston, offers community with communications. With the "commons" metaphor, geographic imagery enters into a nongeographic "global village" medium. "The Commons" evokes the ancient human idea of shared space and links it with the simplicity of orientation in the traditional New England town.

A simple image belies the complex weave of sectors found on a public electronic networking system. Business, education, entertainment and consumer areas coexist and overlap. Each successful application adds to the diversity of the whole network and increases its attractiveness for new applications.

Upper and lower boundaries are easily established in an overview of the developing electronic networking industry. At one end of the spectrum are people, personal computer users, interactive participants—each of us, one by one. At the other end, the large-scale bound, is the global system, the total of all of us and our social sets.

Intermediate aggregation is less obvious. A regional system, such as The New England Commons, provides sufficient size and diversity to become metabolically independent in the American economic environment, while small enough to be distinct and acquire coherence. Myriad "local" systems—local meaning specific, smaller-scale geographic, corporate, institutional, or special interest networks—are accessible through the regional gateway.

Boston is an international city. A Boston/New England network exports information products. People throughout the world use The Commons to connect with the people of New England and its varied resources. We think that the eventual global electronic networking system will emerge as a patchwork of interconnected, large-scale regional systems.

Through electronic networking, we can think and act locally and globally.

Electronic education

One of the earliest US computer conferencing systems is the nonprofit Electronic Information Exchange System (EIES, pronounced "eyes") designed by Murray Turoff. For the first three years of its development, EIES was supported by grants from the US National Science Foundation (NSF). Thus much of the system's early experimentation involved professionals from a number of disciplines who used computer conferencing as a way to exchange information within their fields of study. Electronic communities were formed in such areas as devices for the disabled, social-network analysis, office automation, medical applications and legislative research.

EIES began experimentally in 1976, expanded greatly with increased NSF funding in 1977, and went through yet another change in 1980, when the NSF operational trials ended and the system had to become self-supporting. Using terminals or personal computers in their homes or offices, members of the system are able to hold conferences over long periods of time that simulate but do not duplicate "in-person" conferences. Each conference has its own moderator, and participants are able to add comments, references, papers and any other information that is pertinent to the topic of discussion. Overall, the effect is something like an open microphone at a conference that never ends—a microphone that picks up both formal and informal presentations and discussions.

In addition to providing computerized conferencing facilities, EIES is also an electronic mail service, allowing users to send private messages to one another. Since everything that happens on EIES is stored in the computer, physically situated at the New Jersey Institute of Technology, in Newark, messages can be sent at one time and received whenever the addressee next signs on to the system. Communication is synchronous, when both parties are using the system at the same time, and asynchronous, when messages are sent and retrieved at different times.

When we "signed on" to the system for the first time in 1980, we perused the list of others who were using EIES at that moment and noticed the name of Steve Johnson, one of our postal and telephone friends whom we met through the network research. We sent him a message: "Hello, Steve. Here we are on EIES. How are you and what did you have for breakfast?" A few minutes later a response headlined "How about them cookies?" came back to our bold first message. Johnson welcomed us to EIES and invited us to participate in an EIES conference he was planning a few weeks thence in Seattle. With the Neighborhood Information Sharing Exchange (no longer in existence), Johnson was planning a demonstration of the system at the Seattle CityFair, a huge exposition on urban alternatives. A number of EIES participants were forewarned, and the demonstration happened over a period of days. Each day, Johnson sent a report of what was happening at the CityFair to the group he had invited to participate in the temporary conference on EIES. Johnson introduced a new comment into the conference whenever people came by his booth at the fair requesting information that the disembodied EIES participants might have. EIES members spread out around the world then responded with information "online."

As the communities on EIES have developed and expanded, and people have moved in and out of the system, the EIES world has also grown and changed, much as a geographically based community might, complete with oldtimers, newcomers, and visitors. One "conference" on EIES is called "The Poetry Corner," an ongoing scroll for people to inscribe their thoughts in verse. Another conference is called simply "Graffiti" and contains various bits of wall-written wit, as well as jokes, riddles and rhymes. Often when EIES members have the opportunity, they take a portable computer to "real life" conferences and demonstrate the system to those who are interested.

Four years later, in November 1984, we joined several dozen people on four continents for a month-long study and discussion of networking using EIES.

This course was one in a series offered by the School of Management and Strategic Studies at the Western Behavioral Sciences Institute in La Jolla, California. The two-year program combines semiannual week-long face-to-face seminars with online (the time one is connected to the electronic world) instruction. Rather than leave their regular place of employment to continue their training, these people stay put, and do their travelling electronically.

Each month, different faculty give the online "lectures" and lead discussions on topics in which they are "experts."

We were faculty for the networking course. The students were a mix of corporate, government and nonprofit executives.

Our intention in the course was to introduce networking as a form of organization, distinct from bureaucracy and hierarchy, and as a perspective on the world.

The participants were skeptical. They probed where our thinking was weak, and contributed their own experiences. Drawing on their own interests and from their organizations, the participants drew out examples that illustrate the applicability of networking to large-scale organizations and the connection to small-scale, personal networking.

We select one thread of many to reproduce here, eleven comments out of more than 200 entered during our month course. Known to us as "the Ed Glenn sequence," these comments trace our interaction over three weeks with one participant, Edward P. Glenn, III, a horticulturalist with the Environmental Research Laboratory in New Mexico.

One of the most difficult parts of the online experience to communicate is how *personal* the exchange can be. Even more remarkable is how the very personal and very abstract weave so closely together in the fast-paced spacetime of a rolling conference.

[A few days after the course begins, we attempt to stir things up a bit by pointing to what Virginia Hine wrote about this very group.]

C349 CC1853   Lipnack/Stamps (J & J, 670)   11/6/84
KEYS:/HINE PAPER/GLOBAL MANAGEMENT/
   Virginia Hine's SPIN paper (see Chapters 1 and 9) is an eyebrow raiser. In it, she attempts to explain how the whole world is organized. Words implying forms of organization are highlighted in ALL CAPITAL LETTERS:
   "The four major SEGMENTS of the GLOBAL management NETWORK are upper LEVEL decision makers in MULTINATIONAL CORPORATIONS, in INTERNATIONAL financial INSTITUTIONS, in the GOVERNMENT of both industrialized and underdeveloped 'host' COUNTRIES, and representatives of powerful FAMILIES in Europe, the Americas, the Middle East, South Africa, the Philippines and Asia."
   Some, she says, describe the emergent global management form as an oligarchy, meaning government by the few, specifically, according to the OED, twenty when it comes to botany (oligandrous means fewer than twenty stamens), and four when it comes to language (oligosyllabic means fewer than four syllables).
   The heritage of these modern forms of management is the Arabian desert tribes who practiced fratricide then united to confront the outsider.
   She cites the size of these pre-industrial networks in the hundreds of thousands.
   Is she right? Does her schema describe your organization? Do you attach numbers to your units of responsibility? What are the boundaries between the informal networks and formal lines of authority?

[Five days later, a student comes back with what appears to be a complete putdown of Hine, and challenges us to talk about the dark side of networking.]

C349 CC1867   Edward Glenn (399)   11/11/84
KEYS:/VIRGINIA HINE'S PROPHECIES/
   J & J,

I enjoyed your description of Virginia Hine [not included here]—it's always nice to know the person behind a piece of writing. In her writing she claims the "new age" paradigm recognizes two levels of reality as opposed to the single objective reality of the scientific-industrial paradigm. However, I find much of her prophesy to be mere wishful thinking rather than reality of any kind.

Her type of prophesy is familiar to us now—make a big claim, such as the "dawning of a new age," support it with emotional appeal and anecdotal evidence, and disparage those who hold on to the old, outdated paradigm. One begins to weary of these prophets, with their social jargon mixed with pseudo-science (example: Hine claims the probabilistic nature of quantum theory somehow justifies her belief that networks are the organizational form of the future).

Doubtless the network phenomenon has a kernel of truth. I am grateful to you two for introducing me to this latest version of immortal truth. However, we should look for the down side of networking if we want to be complete. Reading Hine I was struck by the obvious use of networking organizational structure by terrorist organizations such as the IRA and the PLO. Would you care to address this darker side of the human potential/networking movement?

Ed Glenn

[It's a question we've been asked to address before: what about the "bad" networks? Jeff is ready to answer it.]

C349 CC1869 Lipnack/Stamps (J & J, 670) 11/12/84
KEYS:/HINE/DARK VALUES/PROPHECIES/

Thanks, Ed, for your once-again cutting to core issues (cc1867). It is certainly true that networks are not always held together by what I think of as "good" values, which I am sure include some values you and I would agree upon and some not. While we have not studied them, we agree that the "international terrorists" are a good example of a network structure. The Union of International Associations, using a network definition, includes the Mafia in its list of distributed multinational organizations. A moment's reflection about almost any revolutionary movement, from the American, to Russian, to South African, to Solidarity, will bring up images of segmented, semi-autonomous small groups (cells), linked by shared ideology and polycephalous leadership.

In pointing out that networks cohere through relations, values, we are saying that the value content itself can be anything that turns people on. Networks cohere through "normative" power, in Weber's taxonomy, in contrast to "coercive" or "instrumental" sources of power. When a network's integrative ideology begins to swallow its parts (people or groups), the pathology is mob (mass) behavior. A second, quite common, pathology is of the opposite sort, where the value bond is weak or unclear, and the network is impotent or dissolves.

Hine's "new age" paradigm shift certainly suffers from its early 1970s terminology. However, despite what some early writers thought (not including Hine), networking is not only a "human potential" movement, but rather emerges in response to a much more fundamental shift from material to information reality. A few years ago, "the information age" was gee-whiz stuff; now it's old hat. The economic and technological correlates of this "new information age" tell only part of the story of the associated evolutionary changes.

Harlan's [Cleveland, another faculty member] new comment in the leadership conference provides an excellent argument for now being "the twilight of hierarchy." Asserting that the "inherent characteristics of physical resources . . . encouraged the development of hierarchies," Harlan suggests that now that reality increasingly consists of "information resources," "we see vertical pyramids being replaced by consultative committee-work . . . less on orders down . . . more on consent-building."

[A few days later, without having responded to the "Dark Values" message, Ed poses a new line of questioning and Jessica responds.]

C349 CC1889   Edward Glenn (399)   11/15/84
KEYS:/LIMIT OF WRITTEN WORD/
   J & J,
   Could you comment on the limitation that the written word imposes on teleconferencing? Didn't Marshall McLuhan predict that we would be freed from reading and writing in the new age? If information overload is a problem for a

literate group such as this, how can we expect teleconferencing
to become a primary means of communication?

I would be interested to hear your idea of the "ideal" media
for networking (even if it has not yet been invented). In your
work with networks, what is the most common way the
members stay in touch? In person, telephone, mail?

I have found this WBSI course to be a sore test of reading
and writing skills. That's all to the good since this is an
educational network. But I wonder how the personal computer
can be regarded as a "liberating" technology as long as it
demands literary skills for participation.

C349 CC1899   Lipnack/Stamps (J & J, 670)   11/17/84
KEYS:/IDEAL NETWORK MEDIUM/TYPING
TEMPORARY/

Ed,

Re the limitations on teleconferencing of the written word:

Obviously, this medium favors first those who can type and
then very quickly those who can write.

But I think this is temporary: in addition to the Japanese
pictograph-to-abc translation, there's also the words-to-
pictures translation going on.

I think the language of this medium will evolve too. The
useful computer language would combine spoken and written
words with pictures and video and music and data.

My ideal networking technology would allow me to index
all my communication and work. It would connect with my
photos and all our writing, our files, our tapes, our calendar,
and the telephone, in person, and mail traffic through our lives.
It would be portable, such that when we speak our info would
be online and we could add as we go along.

But I don't pine away for this, and I feel quite grateful for
the unimpeded access I have to some very remarkable tools
even now.

On most common ways of staying in touch: it depends.
There are telephoners, writers, and others who prefer to make
the rounds in person.

Our Japanese book translators told us they never write
letters. If at all possible, they visit. Next best is telephone.

There are some very effective networks that never use the

telephone, using the mail exclusively, while still others use neither phone nor mail and base their connections completely on their face-to-face meetings.

And now we have the electronic phenomenon which is both letter, telephone, and in person but really none of these.

Re: viewing this as a "liberating" technology: I'm reminded of the famous futurist we know who will have nothing to do with computers. She says she may get one when they're truly voice-activated because she cannot type. I still think being taught to type when I was 12 was the most important educational experience of my life.

Jessica

[A week after raising the topic, Ed returns to it, and asks, Isn't Lebanon a network nation?]

C349 CC1902   Edward Glenn (399)   11/18/84
KEYS:/LEBANON IS A NETWORK NATION/
    J & J,
I've been following the networking discussion with great interest. There seems to be agreement that networks, if not new, will anyway take on new meaning as the facilitating technologies described by Chuck House [another participant] are developed. Thus Don's [Straus, another participant] concern about the When and Where is especially relevant.

Gerlach and Hine are quite clear that they expect networking to *replace* hierarchical and bureaucratic forms. I think you hold the same hope that networks and shared global values will help us avoid nuclear war. I wish I could agree—certainly networks offer ways to explore issues person-to-person in ways unavailable through official channels. Walt Robert's [another faculty member] call for US-Russian teleconferencing on nuclear winter is an example of how networking can help.

But I don't think networking is a good way to organize nations. When I think of a Segmented, Polycephalous, (Ideological) Network Nation, Lebanon leaps to mind. This state "solved" its factional problems after WWII by organizing a complex net of the various religions and factions, each retaining a degree of sovereignty and military power. This organization worked until challenged by outside forces; then, as we have seen, the country fell apart.

I remember my own involvement as a bit player in the New Left of the 1960s in our own country. The intense factionalism and dogma finally drove me away from that type of political involvement. Had by some misfortune our efforts at "revolution" succeeded, I have no doubt we would have created a nation similar to Lebanon.

Hine lays down the ground rules for a successful network movement [in Gerlach and Hine's *People, Power, Change*]. The movements must be opposed to some aspect of the establishment to bind its members together; ideological debate is necessary to keep the movement segmented and polycephalous; and individuals must experience a conversion process, a "cosmic tap on the head," that seals their commitment. I realize these organizing principles apply to worthwhile organizations as well as the bad. But aren't we being cynical to accept these principles as the best human nature can offer, calling as they do for the suspension of individual responsibility and thought in favor of an ideology (of whatever persuasion)?

Aldous Huxley wrote that social movements always fail to realize that the ends do not justify the means; rather the means determine the ends. Thus if we organize ourselves into factions for the purpose of preventing war, we are really guaranteeing factional disputes and hence war in the long run. Do the network movements described by Hine seem as attractive as ends as they do as means?

[We respond the next day and reject the idea that Lebanon is a SPIN.]

C349 CC1904   Lipnack/Stamps (J & J, 670)   11/19/84
KEYS:/NEITHER EXTREME/NETWORKS ARE MEANS/

Ed, we are glad the networking thread is holding your interest. We hope it is clear by now that we do *not* expect networks to *replace* hierarchy and bureaucracy. Subsume them, yes, but replace them, no. There will always be need for dominance and policies.

Lebanon is not a great example of a SPIN. Although our history in this region is rusty, Lebanon itself is not a very old nation, is it? Weak ties to a new nation, conceived by departing

111

colonial powers, by segments oriented to religions millennia old—unbalance in favour of the parts.

At the other extreme, you object (quite rightly) to a form that calls "for the suspension of individual responsibility and thought in favor of an ideology"—unbalance in favor of the whole.

Networks are about the dynamic interaction of whole and part, neither totally obliterating the other. Where strong parts threaten a weak whole (Lebanon), work on the whole. Where weak parts seem overwhelmed by the whole (movements), work on the rights and power of the composing people and groups.

Look more closely at the Hine review. It is *personal commitment* that is generated by an act of opposition to the established order, *or* one's previous place in it—i.e., any significant personal change. Successful networks most certainly do not have to be opposed to the establishment: witness the electoral landslide led by the polycephalous conservative/fundamentalist/single-issue movement.

Huxley is exactly right that it is the means that determine the end. Thus, we can support the value of networking itself, whatever the networker's/network's values, because the *means* involves horizontal relations between peers based on trust. Ultimately, more participatory means will result in a more participatory world.

    J & J

[Ed does some homework, and three days later, teaches us a lesson. This untitled message is the first political translation of the SPIN that we've seen.]

C349 CC1909 Edward Glenn (399)   11/22/84
    J & J,
    I do think Lebanon is a good example of a SPIN. I happened to read Hine's and the J. C. Penney articles ["Networks: a matrix for exchange," J. C. Penney, *Forum*, March 1983] on networking right after browsing through *The republic of Lebanon, nation in jeopardy* (David Gordon, Westview Press) in the library. Gordon's description of Lebanon's government seemed exactly like Hine's SPIN.

    Lebanon has had a constitution since 1926 but has only

been independent since 1943 so in a sense it is a new nation
as you said. But the major sects that make up Lebanon have
lived together for centuries. Power is shared among the
Christians (Maronites, Greek Catholics, Armenian Catholics,
Roman Catholics, Gregorian Orthodox, Greek Orthodox,
and Nestarian Assyrians), Muslims (Sunnites and Shi'ites),
Druze (a separate religion) and other sects numbering twenty-
two in all. Gordon describes how the sects are organized:
"Each of these forms one or another of the tesserae of what
is sometimes called the Lebanese mosaic; the dynamic by which
each acts as a unit and interacts with the others is usually
termed 'confessionalism' or 'sectarianism' (ta'ifiya in Arabic)."
Each sect is usually organized as an extended family.
"Lebanon is a small place, and these families have had long
experience with each other and with the rules and practices
that makes coexistence possible." Is this not the S in SPIN?

The P in SPIN is guaranteed by the constitution of 1926 and
traditions arising thereafter. The president is always a
Maronite; the prime minister is a Sunnite; the president of the
assembly is a Shi-ite; and cabinet posts and assembly seats
are apportioned to the sects according to the 1932 census
(unfortunately long out of date and one of the points of
dissension in the current struggle). Polycephalous leadership is
further promoted by separate militia maintained by some of
the sects.

Hine defines the I in SPIN as the shared values that keep a
network together as well as the ideological differences that
keep it polycephalous and prevent one node from dominating
the network. This description fits Lebanon in spades. The
binding glue is made of many ingredients. The ruling families
have often banded together against outsiders such as the
French and Turks; they have a common business network that
made the country prosperous before the 1975 civil war (Beirut
was then the Paris of the Middle East); literacy is the highest
in the Middle East including Israel (86 to 84 percent,
according to Gordon based on 1968 data); in general, the
Lebanese are united by the desire for an independent, free-
enterprise state similar to Switzerland.

The ideological differences (ignoring religion) are numerous
but often boil down to how much of an "Arab face" she

should turn to the world: how hard should she fight against
Israel; how much support to give the PLO; should she turn
to the West or East for military support. Recall Hine's
description of the schismatic nature of SPINs which she
illustrated with the example of the Friends of the Earth spinning
off from the Sierra Club. Then think back to the chaos of the
reconciliating meeting among the Lebanese factions last summer
[1984] in Geneva. Doesn't this capture the I in SPIN?

The network structure of the Lebanese government has been
widely blamed as part of the problem there. The government
works well in tranquil times but generally fails to unify to fight
internal or external threats. I have no solutions to offer. The
US and other members of the multinational force tried to
modernize the army and government so Lebanon could
compete against her more modern, aggressive neighbors but
we apparently failed.

Gordon wrote: "Lebanon has been a laboratory for
ethnologists and other students of multiethnic
existence—even if only as a negative model—this in a world
concerned with coexistence on a global scale, with reconciling
and integrating diverse peoples into legitimate, pluralistic
combinations. Perhaps Lebanon may serve only to show what
to avoid; more optimistically, it may show that multiethnic
coexistence is possible, even with internal flaws, unless
destroyed by extrinsic forces."

One negative example such as Lebanon does not prove that
SPINs will not work in organizing our "global village". Now
that I know about SPINs I will be looking for positive examples
as I watch the evening news. My tentative conclusion is that
what makes SPINs strong as vehicles of dissent may make them
weak when they finally achieve power. But I would be happy
to be convinced otherwise.

Happy Thanksgiving!

[Wow!]

C349 CC1914   Lipnack/Stamps (J & J, 670)   11/23/84
KEYS:/LEBANON SPIN/INTERNATIONAL NETS/

Ed, thank you for your thoughtful CC1909. You certainly
have demonstrated for us that Lebanon is a good example of
a SPIN, even if not a successful nation. Examples of networks

5

not working help us extend our understanding of this form and aid us in designing networks more consciously.

Of the three characteristics—Segmented, Polycephalous and Ideological—the binding glue seems the weakest element of the Lebanese network government. This ingredient is clearly the most volatile in the networking mixture: too little in common and the whole can't cohere; too ideological and the whole overwhelms the parts. Here, the ideologies identifying the distinct segments, essentially religious, seem so much sharper and distinct than the Lebanese desire for independence and a free-enterprise state. Your tentative conclusion that what makes a SPIN strong in dissent may make it weak in power is probably correct and related to the ideological role.

One dimension the Lebanon example offers is the variety of ways that segmentation may occur. Segmentation based on religion may make coherence more difficult than segmentation based on region—e.g., US states or Swiss cantons. As we suggested in another comment, the US Constitution can be interpreted as reflecting a network design in the functional segmentation of executive, legislative and judicial power— powers to be balanced, no institution dominating the others.

It may also be that a network may not be the best way to organize a nation (intra-nation), because self-identity is so difficult to achieve in a decentralized form. It may, however, be the best way for the globe to organize itself inter-nationally. In historical terms, bureaucratic organization parallels the rise of the nation-state. Large-scale networks are appearing as the volcanic nation-making process subsides and the inter-nation integration process accelerates.

Indeed, given that the bulk of the world's states are quite resolutely hierarchically organized, we think a meta-state would have to be of the network form. National hierarchs would not tolerate being dominated by a global hierarch. Sovereignty becomes not an impediment to world government, but rather the statement of independence, segmentation, of nations. Absolute sovereign rights, however, would have to go the way of most industrial-age absolutes.

J & J

[And a few days later, Ed sends us a gift of turtles, just as the course is about to end.]

C349 CC1926   Edward Glenn (399)   11/27/84
KEYS:/NETWORKING IN MEXICO/
  J & J,
  I would like to share a networking peace story. It is about my friend Carlos Nagel, a private consultant for US institutions wishing to work in Mexico. We at ERL [Environmental Research Laboratory] do a lot of work in Mexico and over the past four years Carlos has helped us in countless ways. Once a year Carlos and I travel through Mexico together visiting salinized farms at the request of the Mexican forestry research department. During this week-long car ride we share our life stories (several times). Carlos has talked about networking before but until your month I paid him no mind. As part of my networking education last week I bought him lunch and was repaid with the following story.
  "I first started networking in Mexico without knowing what I was doing. I spent four years as the Mexico desk at the Arizona-Sonoran Desert Museum. My work included everything from obtaining collecting permits for rare species to promoting environmental causes in Mexico. I spent the four years traveling throughout Mexico, making contacts at all levels of the government and the private sector. Two things struck me: first, I could get cooperation person-to-person that could not be had institution-to-institution; second, the middle-management level is where the work is done in Mexico.
  "My interest in Mexico grew as the Museum's faded so I finally left to start my own consulting firm. About this time I read *The Aquarian Conspiracy* and discovered I was a networker in Mexico. (I had a similar experience earlier. I spent six years managing a monkey colony in a corner of Puerto Rico. My workers were local fishermen but I soon had them managing the colony by themselves. A year after leaving, I was spending the night with a psychologist and his wife; browsing over his bookcase filled with books on Theory Z and Participatory Management, I discovered what I had done in Puerto Rico.)"

116

Carlos then learned a hard lesson about the fallibility of hierarchies.

He became a consultant for World Wildlife Federation (WWF), headed by Russell Train (ex-Carter cabinet member). They were trying to monitor the breeding grounds of the sea turtles in Michoacan, Mexico. The hawkbill and other turtles lay their eggs on these once-deserted beaches. Today they are threatened by hunting pressure. The turtle meat is prized as food; the eggs as an aphrodisiac; and the oil is put in face cream and sold on the vanity market (much of it in the US).

Mexico has the laws to protect the turtle but the Fisheries Department does not enforce them. Their loyalty is to the fishermen who depend on turtles for cash. The World Wildlife Federation dealing institution-to-institution was unable to convince the Fisheries Department to accept its program for protecting the breeding grounds. Carlos says:

"Really, everyone involved was ready to start doing something about the destruction of turtles. The fishermen wanted a sustained yield, not a slaughter. The Fisheries Department only wanted to help the fishermen. Even the owner of a local turtle processing plant ultimately saw the value in protecting the resource. But the World Wildlife Federation and their man on the scene were more interested in controlling the situation than in working with the Mexicans—they insisted on having their own observers, refusing to relinquish control to Mexican environmental groups; this even though we had created an on-the-scene network whose nodes were the Mexican Marines, the governor of the state of Michoacan, and student observers from the University of Michoacan who were standing by to assist a truly Mexican effort. WWF couldn't accept that the US role was to point out the problem for the Mexicans to solve. They couldn't see that a visible US presence would poison the efforts of the concerned Mexicans.

"The hierarchical WWF in the end was ineffective. Despite their fund-raising ability they couldn't influence the situation in Mexico. I am now resurrecting the network of participants in Mexico—the fishermen, Fisheries Department, university students, plus private sector environmentalists such as Brianda Domeq, author and heir to the Domeq vineyards. The network includes US citizens as well, but this time the relationships will be person-to-person. I believe 'networking', connecting the interested parties who may not even know of each other's existence, will succeed where institutions failed."

Carlos is a dedicated man, a believer in networks and sea turtles, and I wish him well. His company is Intercultural Development Associates in Tucson, Arizona. Next week we take our yearly car ride together and I look forward to sharing what I've learned from J & J this month.

Thank you.

C349 CC1930   Lipnack/Stamps (J & J, 670)   11/29/84
KEYS:/CROSS-CULTURAL NETWORKING/
KEYS:/LONG ROAD TO THANKS/

Ed,

We're very appreciative of your networking peace story about Carlos Nagel's efforts to protect the Michoacan sea turtles. We receive many inquiries about the cross-cultural transportability of networking; this is an excellent example.

When you take your drive with Carlos next week, could you ask him if he'd mind whether we recount his story in our journal?

And, we want to acknowledge your contribution to the development of thought in this course.

Before we started this course, one of our "colleagues" over in the faculty "lounge" took us aside, and briefed us on the students.

"Watch out for Ed Glenn," he said. "If there's anything weak or shoddy in your thinking, Ed will find it."

So it was with great trepidation that our fingers engaged the keyboard, wondering where our feeble minds would reveal themselves.

We've covered a lot of ground since your first challenges in the early part of the month, and want to thank you for helping us cross some new boundaries in our work.

Your examples have been superb, and we request your permission to cite you in our writings.

With thanks,

J & J

The year 2000

A 1980 survey published in *The Wall Street Journal* reported that, within most bureaucratic organizations, only about one in ten people is willing to use a computer. Among the generation that has seen computers develop in two brief decades from multimillion-dollar vacuum-tube behemoths that filled large rooms to powerful "computers-on-a-chip" so small that dozens can be held in the hand, this attitude toward computer use is readily understandable. We wonder what a survey done in 1910 would have indicated about the automobile? Would more than one in ten people have said they could envision themselves driving a car as a daily necessity? Similarly, we wonder what a *Wall Street Journal*–like survey would indicate if taken in the year 2000, when today's children, who have grown up with computers and "intelligent toys" all around them, come of age.

We think of our own children. Our daughter Eliza, at this writing in first grade, is learning how to spell with a small laptop computer. And our older daughter Miranda, when still a preschooler, knew which piece of equipment was the computer and which was simply the typewriter, distinctions that to a less astute observer would appear meaningless since the two pieces of equipment had similar keyboards. Miranda knew that "run" is a word that makes the computer go, as well as being a description of one of her favorite activities.

Our children have been born into a world totally different from that which we were born into during the years in and around the dropping of the first atomic bombs. Our generation seems to have been born to be connected together in this world, with each of us bearing the responsibility for what to do in this awesome moment of transition, predicament and potential that faces us.

CHAPTER 8

Global mind

> Lo, soul, seest thou not God's purpose
> from the first?
> The earth to be spanned,
> connected by network.
>
> Walt Whitman   *Passage to India*

In the year 2001, the turning of a century and the turning of a millennium, our daughters will be 21 and 23.

Once, when we were the age they will be then, we tried to imagine what the future would be like. But no longer.

Rapid, transforming change is no longer an idea grasped by talking to grandparents about 5-cent cups of coffee or looking at old photographs of horseless carriages. Accelerating change is now measured by each of us at least yearly. Where our personal knowledge is greatest, related perhaps to work or a hobby, the pace of change seems faster still and may be measured in months, weeks, and even days. Without knowing what they will be, we do know that the changes from 1980 to 2000 will be more numerous and more astonishing than the changes between 1960 and 1980.

Yet our failure as parents to imagine the future that will greet our daughters as they step into their young adulthood is not simply a shrug of the shoulders and a mutter that no prediction can stand up to the pace of change. Rather, we have recognized that our children's future is, above all, a matter of our *choice*. Mirtala perceives this in a poem accompanying a photograph of her sculpture "The ever-present past," in her book *Thought Forms*:

> I know, my descendant,
> your destiny depends
> on my victories,
> joys, and misfortunes,
> on how I embroider
> my days and years.

It is not the technological surprises, or shifting social patterns, or sudden political events that make it so difficult to forge a vision of the future. Rather, it is the degree of conscious choice that human beings have with regard to the path we take to the future. We know one path leads to Armageddon, and we know other paths lead to slow decline and death. Even forgetting the probabilities of catastrophe, we know that one person's idealized, squeaky-clean future, all white and shiny with spaceships and benevolent bureaucracies, is another person's image of ticky-tacky boxes and omnipresent Big Brother. Similarly, one person's appropriate lifestyle may be another person's version of the Dark Ages.

Future making

Glowing with the shining light of the finest intellectual achievement of the human mind, one small bomb the size of a human body fused the scales of atomic matter and global civilization, the microcosm and the macrocosm. When the Enola Gay released its deadly cargo over Japan in 1945, humankind suffered a loss of ignorance about unseen nature and a loss of innocence about our own evolution. Humankind is now many decades past the point of no-return in accepting the reins of its own destiny in the cosmos.

Mushroom clouds are the ultimate bogeymen of our time. It may be true, as Bertrand Russell said, that we humans have always enacted the follies of which we are capable. Such acts are generally laid at the feet of politicians, but it really was science, through its standard bearer physics, that lost its purity in 1945. Nuclear knowledge and decision making, once the sole province of the princes of science, instantly went to the center of world political consciousness. It sits there still, dominating the great gray area between global war and peace.

Signals of dramatic change are not always so explosive as the Hiroshima and Nagasaki "demonstrations." Yet, turns in the course of human evolution still may arrive with astounding swiftness. Genetic engineering, a product of the 1970s, is one such example, made possible by discoveries several decades earlier about the structure of DNA. In 1980, an infant company—in an untried field and still many months away from a commercial product—sold out its first stock offering within hours. The faculty and trustees of Harvard University wrestled with their academic consciences about whether to form a profit-making partnership with another company jumping into the same unknown waters. Although consequences are as yet unknown, no one—scientists, politicians, or just plain folks—doubts that genetic engineering will profoundly shape the human future.

Genetic engineering is a perfect example of how events poke holes into the very worldviews that give birth to them. A crowning achievement of experimental science dedicated to reducing complexity to elementary pieces, so literally exemplified in snipping and splicing units of life's own information code, genetic engineering brings the reality of evolutionary self-responsibility right to the heart of the human experience. Born of a scientific worldview that perceives evolution as a process of accidental mutations, competitive natural struggle, and very long time frames, genetic engineering itself constitutes an emergent shift in the biological evolutionary process that is totally outside the context of Darwinian explanation.

Men and women acquired powers in the 1970s that humans had always considered godlike. Evolutionary historians of the future will mark that decade as a biological watershed, the moment when humankind began to create life-forms that never before existed on earth. We are, starting right now, taking a hand in our own biological evolution.

As the human responsibility for our own evolution increases, we need perspectives that place humankind and our planet in a larger context. While we can never be certain of the nature of the larger system that includes us all, it is imperative that we persist in stretching our mental models beyond today's transient truths in order to better understand what we do know.

We are two people among 5 billion.
What does that mean?
Can a person grasp a planet? Can a planet know a person?

Stand with us here, in a field on a mountaintop in the Adirondacks, a spot where we feel particularly in tune with the universe, watching the weather boil over purple peaks. Close your eyes and step outward. Change your scale of perception with us, so that we may find a comfortable perspective in which to place our planet and ourselves.

Step outward to the Milky Way, the shimmering necklace of stars ringing the clear night sky. Quickly swing by the sun, pass the giant planets and the outer extremities of our solar system, pass Alpha Centauri and Sirius a few light-years away, and speed 30,000 light-years to our galactic center. Grow and adopt the perspective of Olaf Stapeldon's Starmaker, become the brilliant being that is the Milky Way, a spiraling association of 400 billion suns in a disk 100,000 light-years across.

See, close by, the mini-galaxies making up the Magellanic Clouds, and our neighboring galaxies Sculptor and Fornax, part of our little local group, which extends out about 2 million light-years to include the beautiful Andromeda. Play, then, as part of our local group, with other supergalaxies, such as nearby Virgo, Perseus, Coma and Hydra.

Raise your gaze yet further, and look to the rims of Universe. Stretch your galactic mind to encompass your 100 billion brothers and sisters, each a bright being averaging 100 billion stars.

As ancient Hindu scripture says, it may be that our universe is but an atom in another universe, a mote in another god's eye. But we have gone far enough to recognize our Milky Way as an individual among other galaxies that together form groups in a larger environment of cosmic groups.

So now, returning to the dense core of our own galactic perspective, look outward across your gracefully spinning body, past the Sagittarius Arm, farther out to a back eddy nestled in the Carina-Cygnus Arm, and focus on the small, second-generation star that humans call "the Sun."

As we return our perspective and sense of scale back toward the human home, passing Altair and Procyon and finally Alpha Centauri once again, notice that it is the solar system as a whole that looms in the distance and takes on the appearance of individuality against the relative emptiness of intragalactic space. It is the whole system of star, planets, satellites, comets and encompassing energies that is an entity in the galactic association of solar systems.

Parked outside Pluto's orbit, the Starmaker might wonder about the complexity of this integrated solar animal, 5 billion years old. A glance at the solar subsystems confirms the suspicion of intelligence indicated by the profusion of nonrandom radio signals filling the inner solar space and even now leaking into galactic space. As our perspective narrows to the source of these signals, we approach the third planet.

Although still young, the brain of the solar system, the earth, already has 4 billion neurons and is rapidly growing more. Remarkably, as we zoom in on the pulsing marbled orb that constitutes the seat of solar intelligence and examine one of the billions of elements of this emergent planetary brain, we enter yet another cosmos. Each planetary neuron—a person, a human being—has a brain with something like 10 billion neurons, each neuron capable of perhaps 50,000 connections.

You are home.

Right now the natural limits—smallest to largest—of human networking are at minimum one of us alone and at maximum all of us together—a range from one person to 4-going-on-5 billion people.

Certain large numbers are sometimes breathlessly advanced to illustrate "unimaginable" complexity: neurons in the brain, people on the planet, stars in the galaxies, galaxies in the universe—individuals and billions all. Using a third-grade-arithmetic trick, cancel out all the "billions" and review the cosmic journey:

> Our universe has 100 galaxies,
> Our galaxy has 400 stars,
> Our star system has a brain with 4 people,
> Our body has a brain with 10 neurons.
> Can you hold it in your hand? Universe, sun, and self?

One pair of practiced, globe-holding hands belongs to Robert Muller, Assistant Secretary-General of the United Nations. Muller once described his view of the world to an audience of systems theorists, which he recounts in "A Copernican view of world cooperation:"

> I visualized our globe hanging in the universe and saw it first in its relations with the sun. I viewed it then as an orange cut

in half and saw its atmosphere, its crust and its thin layer of life or biosphere. Within the biosphere, I saw the seas, the oceans, the polar caps, the continents, the mountains, the rivers, the lakes, the soils, the deserts, the animals, the plants, and the humans. Within the crust of the Earth, I saw the depths of the oceans, the continental plates, the underground reservoirs of water, oil, minerals, and heat.

Within the mass of four billion people, I saw the nations, the races, religions, cultures, languages, cities, industries, farms, professions, corporations, institutions, armies, families, down to that incredible cosmos, the human being. In the human person, I saw the rich miraculous system of body, mind, heart and spirit linked through the senses with the heavens and the Earth. I visualized that person from conception to death. I saw the 60 trillion cells of his body, the infinitely small, the atom, microbial life, the incredible world of genes, which embody and transmit the patterns of life.

And all along this Copernican path, at each step, I ask myself the question: "Are humans cooperating on this subject? Are they trying to understand it, appraise it, to see it in relation with everything else?" . . . There is a pattern in all this, a response to a prodigious evolutionary march by the human species toward total consciousness. . . . Something gigantic is going on, a real turning point in evolution.

[I saw us at] the beginning of an entirely new era of which international cooperation at the United Nations was only a first outward reflection. I had not seen it earlier, because it had come in a haphazard way, in response to specific events, needs, crises and perceptions by governments and individuals all over the planet. But the result was now clearly here, glorious and beautiful like Aphrodite emerging from the sea. This was the beginning of a new age, a gigantic step forward in evolution. This was unprecedented and full of immense hope for man's future on his planet. Perhaps after all, we would be able to achieve peace and harmony on Earth. This time, humankind would be forced to think out absolutely everything and to measure the totality of our planet's conditions and evolution in our solar system and in time. The games of glory, aggrandizement and domination by specific groups would soon find their limits. The great hour of truth had arrived for the human race.

Suddenly an image came to my mind. It was the good person of U Thant. He too had foreseen a serene, enlightened world, a world of peace and understanding enriched by ethics, morality, spirituality and philosophy. I remembered the scene of a reception he had offered to the US astronauts after the first moon landing. I was talking in a corner with one of the astronauts. The Secretary-General came near us and inquired what we were talking about. The astronaut answered:

"Your colleague is asking me what I thought when I saw for the first time the entire Earth from outer space."

"Oh, I see," said U Thant. "I am not surprised by his question. But I am afraid he is not expecting anything new from you. He just wants a confirmation, for he has been living on the moon long before you, looking down on Earth with his global eyes and trying to figure out what the human destiny will be."

Vanity of vanities! U Thant was reminding me to take all this with a grain of salt and to return to Earth. My Copernican scheme receded for a moment from my mind and there remained only his enigmatic and kind smile, while the systems analysts were pursuing a discussion which became more and more incomprehensible to me. . . .

Global networking, global mind

Robert Muller was on the original short lists of networkers recommended to us by Robert A. Smith, III (see Chapter 1). We wrote to Dr Muller, mentioning the referral from Bob Smith, explaining what we were up to and requesting information. He responded immediately by sending us a list of US-based international groups associated with the United Nations (non-governmental organizations, or NGOs). Another packet of materials arrived a few days later and yet another a week or so after that. Each packet had a note attached with some scribbled comments about networking, but the third one went on to say, "I think I have so much to say on 'networking' that I will never have time to put it on paper. Perhaps the best solution would be for you to let me know when you next come to New York and we will tape a conversation."

Several months later, we took Muller up on his offer and met him in his modest 29th-floor office at the United Nations. Although at the time, he was head of one of the three principal components of the UN, as Secretary of the Economic and Social Council (ECOSOC) Muller's immediate staff and accommodations exuded all the pomp of a small college dean's office. Muller is the rare kind of unprepossessing person who combines a moving humanity with a wealth of knowledge and a vigorous involvement with the world around him. His own life story, *Most of All, They Taught Me Happiness*, reflects his experiences as a child in Alsace-Lorraine, joining the French underground during the Second World War, being imprisoned, and finally coming to the United States in the late 1940s to work at the UN.

Muller was an extremely easy man for us to interview. He seemed to know exactly why we had come and precisely what we needed to know. He required no leading questions to go directly to the heart of the matter. In essence, his message is this. Humanity is evolving toward a coherent global form best described by the metaphor of a human brain; each person, young or old, able-bodied or handicapped, is an important neuron in the emerging planetary brain that is constituted by the myriad "networkings" among people.

"Networkings", the external connections between people that constitute the internal connections of the planetary whole, is Muller's word. Such phrasings and much of the flavor of his multi-lingual accent have been retained in this interview.

Muller: "This old planet and the human species on it are advancing in time as some kind of a big brain whose neurons are multiplying incessantly, encompassing everything from the individual to the planet, to humanity and the universe, getting deeper and deeper into the past and further and further into the future. Of course, the mathematical interconnections are absolutely staggering. The world brain is already so complicated that you cannot describe it accurately. New interconnections are being created so rapidly that any description would be out of date. This is a new biological phenomenon, one of the most momentous ones in the earth's history. The human species is becoming something new. It is similar to the passage from the protozoa to the metazoa."

Like R. Buckminster Fuller, Muller totally rejects the Malthusian assumption that population growth is the root of human misery. In an evolutionary context, more people potentially means a more complex and more capable planetary brain.

Muller: "We do not even have the faintest idea as to how many people should live on this planet. The question is not even being asked. We are still very primitive when it comes to a transcendence beyond our noses on this little planet and to looking at the mystery of life and what it means to be born and to have life in the immense universe. The fundamental question, the greatest task in being human, and, as a matter of fact, the end goal of all networking, is to try to determine what the laws of the universe are, the cosmic laws which we ought to obey in order to fulfill our lives on this planet and contribute to the further evolution the cosmos has in mind for us.

"The reason Kepler studied astronomy and astrology was to find the laws of the cosmos that would give him clues as to how human societies should live on this planet. The day this will be done, then we will have really entered the new age. We are doing it the hard way, with many mistakes and very partial views instead of having a universal view, not only a global view for the planet but of our total relationship with the universe.

"Now, when you speak about world government, many listeners think that you should have your head examined. When you speak about cosmic government, then you are ready for an asylum! And yet, this is the real, ultimate issue. The question whether we will be blown up in a nuclear holocaust is very much part of it. Did all our long cosmic evolution have as the sole purpose the triggering of an atomic war to assert the righteousness and supremacy of a one power on earth? So we have a very tall order in our lap."

Giving us a thumbnail sketch of the UN's history, Muller began with the golden era of industrialism, the end of the nineteenth century, a time when "dreamers like the steelmaker and pacifist

Andrew Carnegie" envisioned a world order established on a totally rational, scientific, technological and professional basis. In the original scheme, a league of professional associations was to be created on an equal footing with a league of nations, but this idea got lost in the shuffle after World War I. Of course, the "half-a-loaf" League of Nations never got off the ground, because of the absence of the United States. In Muller's words, this is how the current UN came about: "Humpty Dumpty went to the Second World War, after which the world union idea was revived, but the project for a league of professional associations was never really revived as a possible people's democracy at the world level. World organization became a government-owned affair."

Outside the UN's political and legal functions is Muller's realm, a fascinating collection of the world agencies connected to a lattice-work of international networks.

Muller: "I am Secretary of the Economic and Social Council, where everything economic and social is brought together. Under the Charter, we are instructed to have a total worldview: demography, health, education, standards of living, longevity, culture, employment, children, women, the elderly, the hungry, the oppressed, the discriminated, everything you can imagine. The UN is a system of central universal organs with functional and regional agencies hooked into it. People usually do not have the faintest idea what beginnings of a world system exist here. The UN's world conferences on population, on the environment, on energy, on water, on the deserts, and so forth are the big drums being used to give messages and global warnings to people. We are, of course, still living primarily in a rational, scientific age, and this is definitely reflected in the UN. But ethical, moral, and even spiritual considerations are becoming stronger every year. The new ethics of what is right and wrong for humanity, that is really the basic business of the UN behind all the politics and the bureaucracy. It is a very, very difficult task, but we must go through it and work it out. Just another new fundamental biological process.

"Everything good or bad until now has always been decided in terms of what is good or bad for a group or a nation and seldom from the point of view of what is good or bad for the entire humanity. This has become a central question because

129

our survival depends on it. Ecology has recently taught us to ask the question 'What is good and what is bad for our planet?' At every step we must henceforth ask, 'What is good and what is bad for humanity?' A completely new ethic is being born, but it is very difficult, because interest groups cling to their advantages and views: the powerful want to remain armed, the rich want to remain rich, everybody wants more, and few are those who would be ready to give up something for the good of the planet and humanity."

Even as Muller paints pictures of thickening global webs on every issue and topic from avocados to asteroids, the conversation always returns to the emphatic statement that there is no networking, no global brain, no anything without the individual human being. Muller does not see the individual as the unfortunate lowest rung on the ladder of global organization. Rather, humans are the very source and prescient mirror of global complexity.

Muller: "The Indian yogis tell us that each human being is a microcosm of the cosmos. It makes good sense. How could it be otherwise?

"Even a particle, or an amoeba or a hydra, is a self-contained entity, but at the same time it is part of the totality. It is this type of complex relationship, being a whole and a part together, which is again, networking, because all connections together make up the total reality. As an individual, you feel and are an absolutely unique being, never to be repeated exactly the same in all eternity. And yet, you are part of the total universe and total stream of time. As a matter of fact, this shows us the range of human happiness: we can be happy through concentration upon ourselves (know thyself), through networking with others and the wonders of our planet, or through networking with God or the Total-Absolute through spirituality, meditation, and prayer.

"From the moment you have recognized both your entity, and being part of the total human family and universe, from that time you will change and the world will change. But, again, this is a very tall order, one of the hardest philosophical problems of our time. It was a great musician and humanist, Pablo Casals, who gave it the best expression when, with tears in his eyes, he used to exclaim, 'I am a miracle that God

or Nature has made. Could I kill? Could I kill someone? No,
I can't. Or another human being who is a miracle like me, can
he kill me?'

"And to be great and unique, you don't have to be in the
newspapers. Networking, in my view is not necessarily only
the need to 'fight for something', a cause. It can be a serene,
natural association of sorts, from the monk's association with
God in his monastery to people who like to collect stamps.
Networking is a form of happiness. A person can say, 'There
are lots of other people like me,' and you become a little world
of your own: some like astronomy and others like collecting
stamps. It is truly a fantastic life, a beautiful life on this planet
which offers so many possibilities of happiness in every
direction.

"If I were a head of state, I would support networking
because it gives so many people a sense of purpose. Not
everybody can be a mathematician, a scientist, or a
philosopher. Many people are interested only in their little
gardens. But to have one's garden may not be enough. So you
order a gardening magazine and you join a gardening club.
There you meet other people with the same interest, with
whom you can talk about things you love and you derive
much happiness from that network. We are four and a half
billion people on this planet and each wants to be recognized
as 'somebody', as an entity. Even, and especially, when you
are limited or handicapped, you want to be 'recognized'.

"When I feel depressed I read Beethoven's Heiligenstadt
Testament, in which he tells his brother that he is becoming
completely deaf but that he is determined to give the world
what he feels in himself. You tell this to handicapped people
and it gives them courage. Did you know that the Taj Mahal,
in India, was designed by a blind Persian architect, Ustad
Isha? Perhaps someone with sight would have never been able
to design it.

"Once, I was asked to give a graduation speech to a school
for the blind. I asked them to recommend a book which
would speak about the great blind people of this earth
throughout history. I could not believe it when I learned that
such a book did not exist. I exclaimed: 'You have all these
blind children and you do not even have a book about

Homer, Milton, Euler, Ustad Isha, and all other great blind people who have contributed so much to human civilization?' So here again is the need for a network among the handicapped, who need their heroes and recognition of their entity.

"But it is even more; it has to do with transcendence. I'm digressing, but—"

Encouraged to follow his thought, Muller explained his experience of listening to a record of a lovingly crafted autobiographical story he had written called "Happy even in prison" (a chapter in his book *Most of All, They Taught Me Happiness*), made for blind people by the US Library of Congress.

Muller: "With my eyes closed, I listened to that story. I was in a completely different world. I remembered things in that prison that had gone forever. Suddenly I discovered that when your eyes are closed, your mind functions better when it is auditively impressed and I realized that blind people might derive a pride from the extra perception they have by being only auditive.

"As part of the 1981 International Year for the Disabled, I recommended that each nation should honor its great handicapped. National committees federating all handicapped associations were established in each country. There are 450 million handicapped people in the world, and the world must do something about such a sizable problem. So we decided to make a big noise about it, to launch an International Year. Each country reported on the problem to the UN and looked into all aspects of it. The result is that the handicapped have been hooked in on a world scale through the UN. They represent a network of 450 million people.

"A remarkable thing is that we have been able in the UN to have governments work together on a whole gamut of human problems, from childhood to old age. There is UNICEF. We had an International Year for the Child. There were two world women's conferences. There was a world youth conference, several conferences to combat racism. In 1982, there was a world conference on the elderly. I am sure that within a few years there will be a UN conference on the problem of death. All these efforts are aimed at very sizable worldwide networks of people, each with its host of nongovernmental organizations.

"Then there are networks between these various groups, for instance between old people and young people. In Africa and Asia, the aged are the superiors, the wise people, the people to whom the young go for counsel. In the West we put them in old people's homes. I have written a lot about this subject because of my relations with my grandfather. He was such a wise and warm human being. He had no axe to grind, contrary to my father. I could believe my grandfather. He had nothing to lose, but all to offer: wisdom. Today in the West we cut off the elderly from the young, because promoters want to build old people's homes. Thus we prevent an important channel of transmission of wisdom of life to the young. Then the developing countries imitate the great ideas of the West and run into untold problems. As a result, the need for proper networking will never end.

"Networking is done by people who have no networks. That seems to be a fundamental law. Those who have the major networks don't want to engage with those who have new views about humanity. For example, the multinational corporations give the cold shoulder to the UN. Having power, they don't want to network with the international agencies. The big TV stations don't want to network with new-age groups. They have their own monopoly. The *New York Times* doesn't want to network with anyone.

"This is why the voiceless people have begun to find out about networking in order to assert themselves again. It is the old story of humanity: those in power do not want to give up anything, and those who are left out want to organize to be heard. So the UN's greatest allies are generally those who have no great power: the little countries, the innumerable nongovernmental organizations represented by observers to the UN, and the religions. If the Pope had vast military forces he probably wouldn't come to the UN. He has only spiritual power, and this is why he is allying with a weak United Nations sharing the same objectives.

"It is the absence of certain vital networks which causes much of the trouble in this world. There is no real networking between heads of state, an area where it would be so vitally

needed for the survival of our planet; there is no networking
between the military, there is no networking between ministries
of justice and the police forces of this planet. International
terrorists are better organized. Here is where the system breaks
down. In order to keep their advantages, sovereignty and
primacy, the governments of the big nations generally refuse
to network. Roosevelt was a man who knew how to network.
He insisted on seeing Stalin, Churchill and De Gaulle, and he
saw them and communicated with them all the time. He
created a world system of communications, including
cooperation between the military, which broke down after
his death with the policy of the Iron Curtain and the cold
war."

In a paper he showed us, "Proposals for better world security,"
Muller recalls the words of Chou En-lai:

I will never forget a wise and melancholic remark made by
Premier Chou En-lai during the visit of Secretary-General
Waldheim to Peking in 1972: "I am sitting here surrounded
by my advisers trying to figure out what they might be
scheming against us in Moscow and in Washington. In
Moscow, they are trying to figure out what Peking and
Washington might be scheming against them. And they are
doing the same in Washington. But perhaps in reality no one
is scheming against anyone." And he concluded that the role
of the Secretary-General as an intermediary between heads of
states was extremely important. As I listened to him, I closed
my eyes for a moment and visualized the day when in his
large office in the People's Hall there will be an audio-TV set
linked with the offices of his main partners in the administration
of planet Earth.

Muller: "I have worked with a number of Secretaries-General
and I noticed that they all had their private networks.
Hammarskjöld wrote to Albert Schweitzer, asking him to come
up with a resounding statement with other scientists for the
ban of atomic tests. He did it in a private capacity, without
asking the authorization of governments. And it worked. U
Thant was very interested in the UFOs. I never knew about it
and later learned that he had a network of three people who

informed him of everything that was going on in this field. I
assume that people in high positions all have their private
networks.

"Networking operates all the time. You do it as a private
person, you work with people who are like-minded, and this
is quite a force, because the power of ideas is enormous."

For Muller, networking is a way of being fully human.

Muller: "There is more to the art of networking. You really
have to live it, not just passing information on without it
touching you or being touched by you. You are part of the
totality, you are a seeker of truth, of what is good for the
human race, of what will be our fate, of what will improve
our fate. If you are not totally honest, people will not trust
you, they will not believe you. It has to be deeply lived. Then
you are a good networker, a useful neuron which will not be
rejected by the new brain in formation. Most of the time,
people listen to you with the brain, but often you will be able
to convince them only if you speak with your heart to their
heart."

As Muller caught his breath, we asked him one last question.

Muller: "Who are the greatest networkers that I know? That
is a difficult question. I believe that the greatest networkers
are those who did it at the highest or deepest human,
philosophical, moral, ethical and spiritual levels—people like
the Buddha, Jesus, Gandhi, Schweitzer, Teilhard de Chardin,
Martin Luther King, Hammarskjöld, U Thant, people who
really transcended races, nations and groups, and networked
at the all-human level, linking the heavens and the earth and
showing us our prodigious worth and journey in the universe.
People like Bach, Beethoven, Shakespeare, Goethe, who make
us feel the greatness of life and again fuse the heavens with the
earth. They have reached the pinnacle of networking, not the
heads of government of today, who will be completely
forgotten in a few years. Those great people were not
networking during their own times only, but they continue to
network over the centuries into our own times. Their dreams
and thoughts and feelings are still alive today. The real
networkers are those who go deepest and come closest to the

mystery of life in the universe. Of course, these are my great networkers, because I work for the United Nations. For the Catholics probably the Pope is the greatest networker, and for the Rotarians and International Lions their current presidents are the greatest networkers.

"What is really needed today is a new philosophy of life within our global conditions, a new hope, a new vision of the future. And the strange, beautiful thing is that probably this time the vision will not be the product of any one person, but will be a collective product. It will be the creation of the new human species as a macroorganism, as a perfected neural system made up of thousands and thousands of networks. As we move towards the bimillennium, perhaps networking will become the new democracy, a new major element in the system of governance, a new way of living in the global, miraculous, complex conditions of our strange, wonderful, live planet spinning and circling in the prodigious universe at a crossroads of infinity and eternity."

CHAPTER 9

A network model

Constructing a theory about networks is very risky. For the most part, network theory has been based on physical systems that function as networks: communications, information, and transportation systems, just to name a few, all of which have their own theoretical heritages, primarily derived from engineering.

In the people-to-people/group-to-group networks that are the subject of this book, practice has preceded theory. Thus, we have used our personal knowledge and our interpretation of the experience of others to create a "model" of networks, briefly encapsulated in ten aspects or characteristics. We do not now have nor will we ever have the sole "correct" model of networks. What we have is *a* model that for us makes sense out of the mass of material we assembled.

Our model was not created in a vacuum, nor simply from our mail-order materials and personal experience. Some of our correspondents became collaborators in our struggle to understand networks. They wrote letters, sent articles, and recommended books that they thought might be helpful. One article in particular, by anthropologist Virginia Hine, was often mentioned by knowledgeable people, and a number of copies were sent to us. Indeed, Robert A. Smith, III (see Chapter 1) had sent it to us shortly after its 1977 publication in *World Issues*, the magazine of the Center for the Study of Democratic Institutions. In this article, "The basic paradigm of a future socio-cultural system," Hine, whose seminal work on networks has been done in conjunction with anthropologist Luther Gerlach, writes, "Wherever people organize themselves to change some aspect of society, a non-bureaucratic but very effective form of organizational structure seems to emerge.

We called the type of structure we were observing a 'segmented polycephalous network.' "

In four breathtaking pages, Hine identifies three essential qualities of networks. They are (1) *segmented*, "composed of autonomous segments which are organizationally self-sufficient." Networks are (2) *decentralized*, connected by horizontal linkages such as overlapping membership and mobile leadership. And networks are held together through a fabric of (3) *shared values* and unifying ideas, an "ideological bond" that, in Hine's view, is the most important network characteristic. Shared values hold the decentralized segments of a network together in a dynamic pattern of interaction.

Challenging the assumption that bureaucracy and hierarchy are the only viable forms of organization for large numbers of people, Hine points to networks as another, and in many cases a more appropriate, form of large-scale organization. From her outpost on the social frontier, Hine sees networks growing most vigorously at the extreme ends of the scales of power and influence. Networks, she says, are emerging both among the global elite and the powerless everywhere.

If this model has any validity, the organizational structure of the future is already being created by the most as well as the least powerful. It is very clear, however, that the ideologies which inform [networks] at the two levels are diametrically opposed.

In this chapter we present a network model. Our ten-point model may be viewed as simply an extension of the Gerlach/Hine three-point model. We see the same network phenomena that they see, and that many others see. We suspect that most people will find that many of the network characteristics discussed here fit with their own images and ideas about networking.

Our model of networks consists of ten characteristics, five of which describe a network's structure and five of which describe a network's process.

Structure	Process
Holons	Relationships
Levels	Fuzziness
Decentralized	Nodes and Links
Fly-eyed	Me and We
Polycephalous	Values

138

A network model

Each of the ten attributes represents one significant idea about networks and networking; all networks reflect at least one, if not several, of these aspects or characteristics. For us, the overall concept of networks includes all ten ideas working together, creating one general pattern that distinguishes networks from other types of organizations. In our minds, these concepts overlap and interweave into what Bateson called "a pattern that connects."

The structure of networks

(1) Holons

All of life is made up of "whole" things that are also "part" of something else. A network is both a *whole* in and of itself, and a *part* of something larger than itself. A network participant is both a whole in and of it/him/herself and part of something larger—namely, a network. We use the word coined by Arthur Koestler, "holon," meaning whole-part, to describe this interconnected attribute of the world around us.

Life abounds with examples of holons. A person is both a whole individual *and* a part of a family. A family is a whole social unit of relatives *and* a part of a community. A community is a whole collection of individuals and families *and* a part of a country and a world. A person as a whole is also a macro-universe of his/her own, structured in another sequence of holons: a whole body is an integration of many organ parts, human organs are wholes made up of cellular parts, and cells are wholes made up of molecular and atomic parts.

In networks of individuals, people are parts who are recognized as self-sufficient wholes capable of autonomous functioning. At the same time, a person participates—literally, "takes part"—in the "wholeness" of the network that arises from the work of many people. The same concept applies to networks that link groups and organizations: each group is respected for its integrity and independent activities as a whole, while simultaneously being integrated as a part into the larger whole of the network. Judy Norsigian, for example, is a unique person who participates in the Boston Women's Health Book Collective. The Collective, in turn, is a part of the National Women's Health Network, composed of groups and individuals.

139

Virginia Hine uses the word *segmentation* to refer to the holon nature of networks. Describing a network as "a badly knotted fishnet", a web of links between self-reliant nodes, Hine considers segmentation to be one of the three key characteristics of a network. It is precisely this attribute of self-sustaining parts that gives the network form its remarkable resiliency and its adaptability to stress. Segmentation explains why, for example, underground political movements are so difficult to suppress. Squashing one node does little to impair the effectiveness of the net as a whole.

The independence of holons in networks contrasts sharply with the standardized, synchronized, and precisely fitted parts of a bureaucracy that become more dependent as specialization and size increase. For example, while a person like Judy Norsigian can testify at a public health hearing without obtaining "clearance" from any "higher authority," an employee of a health insurance company does not enjoy such autonomy. Of course, no one in a network can be totally self-reliant, and, indeed, a network arises out of needs and visions that cannot be fulfilled in isolation. But by attributing respect to its own parts and supporting the independence of its participants, a network is encouraged to recognize the qualities of autonomy and interdependence at all levels of social interaction.

Because it treats its participants with respect, a network as a whole expects its voice to be treated with respect as it plays a part in a larger whole. Ultimately, the meaning of networks always comes back to people. The principle of holons, of autonomy and respect for participants, is fundamentally a respect for people, a respect for one another's individuality and potential contribution to the whole.

(2) Levels

While networks are not hierarchies, they do reflect the pattern of levels. Just as everything is a holon, so does everything reflect the pattern of levels. A whole is one level and a part is another level. In the same way as atoms, molecules, cells, organs, and organisms are all levels within levels, so are people, groups, organizations and societies levels within levels.

Levels are a useful tool for organizing complex structures, one we use every day to describe the world around us. Governments

140

operate at the local, state and national levels. Currency is composed of levels of values—cents in dimes in dollars. Measuring systems are made up of linear levels—inches in feet in miles. Time is counted in levels of seconds making up minutes which count hours in a day. Information systems are invariably organized in levels, from the Dewey Decimal codes at the local library to the parts of our telephone number (area code + local exchange + our phone). Computer hardware (the machine itself) is built up as a series of levels from simple on-off switches to highly complex "hardwired" logic. Computer software (the programs that tell the machine what to do) is designed in levels of increasingly general "languages"— machine languages, assembly languages, "higher" languages such as BASIC and Pascal, support and management utilities, and, finally, customized application procedures.

So, like everything else in the universe, networks are completely caught up in the pattern of levels. Networks are collectives of friends, organizations of members, coalitions of organizations, and alliances of coalitions. Networks form in neighborhoods to deal with community problems, in regions to deal with global problems, in transnational associations to deal with human problems. Networks are formed in every conceivable combination of social levels—from person to humankind.

Virtually every significant issue motivating the development of the networks on the Invisible Planet has to do with the relations between levels of social organization—global, national, regional, state, local, grass-roots, family, individual. Whether the concern is with health care, ecology, energy, economics, power, personal growth, education, or communications, the networking approach invariably involves the rights, responsibilities and interconnections of the many levels of social decision making. Jack Miller, of Anvil Press, expresses the sentiments of many networkers when he says, "We believe that forming networks is simply a natural outgrowth of our commitment to be responsible members of our community, region, nation, and world."

A network is a whole made up of participant parts. In networks comprising individuals, each participant in turn is the hub of a personal network of family, friends, and contacts. Networks are composed of participants who have friends. This indistinct level of informally connected "friends" of participants is a rarely reco- gnized but often crucial level for understanding the astonishing growth and influence that a small network might exert in a particular situation—an aspect of networking that politicians understand intuitively. Gerlach and Hine describe this as a process of "face-to-face recruitment along lines of pre-existing positive affect relationships." Hine translates from "social scientific-ese":

> Networks expand along these lines not because of media coverage or speeches by charismatic leaders. Too many networkers make the "old age" mistake (a costly one) of thinking they can attract numbers or spread ideas with mailings or flyers, when it is the one-to-one contact that is the basic growth mechanism of a network.

Networks also comprise groups (Gerlach and Hine define the "basic structure for sociocultural change" as a network made up of groups), and networks themselves may form networks. While new networks opening up new issues might think of themselves as alone in the world, many networks articulate important variations on the same general theme. For example, within the renewable-energy field, one network might concentrate on the whole spectrum of solar power, while another network might concentrate on passive solar devices, while still another network might concentrate on underground homes in the context of passive solar technologies. These networks of a feather often flock together as parts of a loosely seen "metanetwork"—a network of networks.

Like other types of organizations, networks reflect a level pattern. We see networks in terms of four levels: a group of *friends* (level 1) includes people who are *participants* (level 2) in a *network* (level 3) which is part of a larger *metanetwork* (level 4).

For the most part, the networks mentioned in this book are level 3 organizations. That is, these networks have some features of collective identity, including at least (a) a group name and (b) a mailing address. A level 3 network may also be identified by having a telephone number, a logo, stationery, flyers, publications, other media, products, offices, and/or a staff. In some cases, these groups operate in hierarchical fashion, with officers and traditional lines of authority, yet their interaction with other, similar groups makes them *nodes* (see below) in the larger network.

There are, of course, numerous level 2 networks, largely undocumentable, usually having a small membership but none or little of the level 3 group-identity paraphernalia. Examples of these would be groups of community, business, or professional friends who share experiences and exchange information. As for level 1, personal networks, most of us have a web of relationships that sustain us (or not) in our daily lives.

A few examples in this book are truly level 4 metanetworks, and there are many substantial fragments of metanetworks in most of the areas covered in our survey. It is our view that there is an increasingly choate metanetwork of shared values among all the extremely diverse networks we have identified as parts of an Invisible Planet. Indeed, we hope that by putting such differing groups together we can help communicate the underlying pattern that connects them all and can contribute to the emergence of a globally/ personally concerned metanetwork. The Invisible Planet is a grand metanetwork, a pattern that connects us to a future of hope for ourselves and our children.

(3) Decentralized

Although networks and bureaucracies both have level structure and are wholes with parts within wholes, networks and bureaucracies differ in how they structure the relationship between the whole and its parts. Bureaucracies tend to bring parts together through *centralized* control and to *maximize* the dependency of parts on the whole. Networks tend to bring parts together under *decentralized* cooperation and to *minimize* their dependency on the whole. Network parts are dispersed and flexibly connected, whereas bureaucratic parts are concentrated and rigidly connected.

Ideally, the forces of distribution and concentration can work together to maintain healthy parts and growing wholes. But in our time it is the tendency to centralization which has gone too far, and it is the process of decentralization which needs development right now.

The statement of principles by TRANET, the Transnational Network of Appropriate/Alternative Technology, explains why they chose the term "network" to describe their organization.

> For governance, "network" implies a non-hierarchical system
> of equal, independent, self-sustaining members. Unlike a
> bureaucracy a network is dependent on no one of its parts.
> No organ performs a specialized task necessary for the

function of the whole. A net has no center. It is made up of links between parts. TRANET's role [is] to strengthen these links. . . . The potentials for the future demand a humanization through decentralization.

TRANET is a whole: there are a name, an office in Rangeley, Maine, a staff, some files, and a vast collective memory bank of personal experience in its chosen field, appropriate technology (AT). Organizationally, TRANET resembles many of its member groups. Within the network, TRANET's role is not control but facilitation. Whereas a bureaucracy invariably has a controlling organ that serves as a decision maker, TRANET and other network hubs function to facilitate cooperative decision making.

A simple mental test can be used to judge whether a particular organization is predominately centralized or decentralized. Just remove the individual or group that functions for the whole.

Imagine TRANET vanishing overnight. The international AT movement would certainly not collapse, nor would any of TRANET's members, although they would likely be somewhat inconvenienced and considerably saddened that a trusted channel of global communication had disappeared. Shortly thereafter, however, another international AT clearinghouse would certainly spring up, or perhaps several, particularly if TRANET happened to explode from internal dissension over goals and means.

By contrast, mentally remove "command central" from an industrial-age institution. The likely result is either paralysis or disintegration, or both. Imagine a bureaucratic army with its headquarters blown away: a helpless, headless, fragmenting giant. Now remember how many times United States aircraft "destroyed" the guerrilla headquarters of the "Viet Cong." The jungle network endured, and won.

According to the Gerlach/Hine model, decentralization is the second major characteristic of networks, a concept that incorporates cooperation with independence. Networks strive for decentralization at every level, an idea that reflects a respect for the integrity and responsibility of people, each and every one of us. In networks, the world now has many experiments in new forms of democratic cooperation.

(4) Fly-eyed

Like the fly whose "one" eye comprises thousands of individual eyes, networks "see" through many perspectives, although the unknowing observer may think they have only one point of view.

At times, a network seems to "see" with one eye and "speak" with one voice, testifying to consensus around an idea or a strategy. Such moments of unanimity are important, because they often reveal the essential common values and bonds that explain the unity among the diversity of network viewpoints.

At other times, a network may appear to be a babble of disconnected concerns and interests, or an arena of internecine warfare. Hine calls this trait "the 'fission-fusion' characteristic that confuses observers and leads the bureaucratically minded to see networks as 'lacking' in organization." Networks not only tend to put up with disagreement, in many ways they depend upon it. The forthright independence of the members keeps the network as a whole from being dominated by any single node. Hine writes that while it is a shared vision that keeps a network together, "it is the conflicting concepts of goals-means that prevent any one segment from taking permanent control over all the others."

Reflecting a structure that requires relatively few people in authority, hierarchies are governed by rigid rules and codes, while bureaucracies keep order through standards and policies. The idea that there could be, or ought to be, one "correct" viewpoint, one authority who "knows best," is certainly consistent with the old-time physics, as well as the old-time religion. But just as the priestly ruler, from whom the word hierarchy is taken, is rapidly receding into history, so is the idea that there is *only one right* point of view.

Where once, BE (before Einstein), educated folk knew for sure that the universe was governed by absolutes of space and time, right and wrong, now we all slip and slide around in a universe of relatives. Einstein shook off the blinders of his schooling in Newtonian mechanics and saw differently. He saw that the meaning of distance, speed and time vary depending on your perspective.

Until the great triumphs of Copernicus, Kepler and Galileo, the conventional Western wisdom had been that the earth was the center of the universe. Everything else in the heavens was explained from our God-given position on terra firma. Early scientists inaugurated a new age of humankind by establishing the sun as the "correct" and "true" center of at least our local heavens. Now even that view is seen as only one of many. The solar system may be understood with a point of reference on the sun, the earth, Pluto, the moon, an orbiting space station, or the star Alpha Centauri. All are valid perspectives.

The many perspectives of a network derive from the autonomy of its members. All have their own turf and agendas, yet they cooperate in the network because they also have some common values and visions. Just as the many points of reference of Einstein's universe are bound together by universal patterns of energy (such as the speed of light), so the many perspectives of a network are bound together by universal patterns of value.

An excellent example of this is manifest in the natural childbirth movement—a loose network of parents, professionals and health-care activists advocating a variety of alternatives to the routine maternity experience. While millions of people associate themselves in some way with the idea of "natural childbirth," sharp differences exist among those who favor medication-free births in the delivery room, those who advocate the use of in-hospital birthing rooms, and those who are working to establish out-of-hospital, free-standing birth centers, all of which are constituencies quite apart from those favoring midwife-attended home births. Although these separate voices disagree as to which strategy will provide the best balance of risk, health and meaningful experience for babies, mothers and fathers, all are in agreement that the high-technology model of childbirth propounded by much of the medical profession must be changed and humanized.

(5) Polycephalous

Networks, like all social organizations, need leadership, whether distributed or centralized. In networks, leadership is "polyce-phalous," to use Gerlach and Hine's term, which literally means "many-heads." Ideally, all the participants in a network share in the leadership functions by taking responsibility for tasks and viewpoints related to the network as a whole. In practice, for the most part, network leadership is plural and porous.

As we pointed out above in the TRANET example, leadership in a network means facilitation, not control. An obvious and frequent problem that plagues contemporary networks is a confusion and conflict between cooperative leadership and singular control. In a telephone interview with us, James Gordon, a physician and an energetic networker, remarked that the biggest problem in networks is power. Big egos. People losing spirit and falling into factionalism. It is hard, he said, to develop good leaders, and it is harder still to know how to deal with them. Hine comments:

> This factionalism, the ego-prickles of leaders, is one of the principal reasons for the spread of a network. Squabbles between leaders in a network often lead to splits so that two nodes appear in the place of one. I had many instances in my files . . . like the "eco-radical" who had a talent for inspiring a one-shot activity and collecting people who would then become a group around his leadership. Invariably, a dispute would arise as he tended to be very authoritarian. The group would fight with him. He would leave in a huff and start something else, leaving a trail of anger/bad vibes behind him but *also* six or eight *viable*, active nodes in the network. Leadership "problems" can be blessings in disguise though they never feel that way at the time.

The issue of leadership, cooperation conflicting with control, is not resolved in networks, as it can never be in any final sense. But in networks, contemporary society has experiments in many-headed leadership to offer as an alternative to the centuries of domination by singular, "top dog" leadership structures.

Polycephalous network leadership is not only cooperative and distributed, Hine points out, but it is also extremely mobile. People who are leaders in one segment of a network can easily serve a facilitating function in another segment of the same network or a different network. A "natural networker," particularly in the younger, "hobo" days, moves around from place to place, entering or starting networks at each stop, relating each new or newly discovered network to the ones encountered before, whether social action or progressive contacts.

The decade-long movement against the American war in Vietnam provides a dramatic example of mobile polycephalous leadership on a massive scale. Leadership sprouted everywhere, appearing and disappearing, incessantly moving, changing from moment to moment. Multiple leadership worked because there was a strong central core of values and assumptions that all members of the antiwar network shared either implicitly or explicitly.

In an active, dynamically growing network oriented to a change in the status quo, leadership may be even more than multiheaded and mobile. When a bureaucracy tries to suppress an unwelcome network, it may find itself confronting the second labor of Hercules. Each time one head was cut from the body of the Hydra, this multiheaded dragon of fable, two heads grew in its place. In multiple-leader networks, new leaders emerge in response to circumstance and need, and two heads will arise to fill a role left by the removal of any one head as needs demand.

The process of networking

(6) Relationships

Networks work because of the dynamic relationships that transpire among the people involved. To understand the process of networking, we have to shift from thinking about *things* and the way they are built to thinking about *relationships* and the way they behave.

Normally, through the conceptual glasses of substance and space, we are tuned to the things of the world, looking for solidity when we sit down and detouring around objects in our way. When we look at networks through the same materialistic glasses, they seem quite invisible. "Networks," writes Johnny Light, a veteran networker originally based in Detroit, "are quite invisible to the eye and difficult to document." But we all know, as futurist Robert Theobald says, "that much of the work in any system is done through informal and invisible networks, rather than through the formal visible authority structures."

Networks seem invisible because so much of the meaning of networks is bound up in relationships: the links, connections, communications, friendships, trusts and values that give the network its life. In a network, the spatial furniture can be quite minimal: a phone, index cards, file drawers, a room in the basement. Try using time-lapse photography magically tuned to the vibrations of human relationships. A network is revealed as having a richly diverse ecology of intertwining patterns and flows.

148

Another image of the visible and invisible worlds beneath our noses is suggested by a flight along the northeast megalopolis corridor from Boston to Washington (BOS-WASH, as the people on the air shuttle call it). In the morning, on the flight south, the structures and fixed patterns of the industrial world fill the window: roads, buildings, football fields, water towers. On the trip north, at night, a wonderous transformation has occurred. There are no asphalt parking lots, nor brick- and-mortar factories, nor geometrically plowed fields. Instead there are ribbons and clusters of light, myriad faint pinpricks in dark spaces between great shimmering seas of urban brilliance—a reality completely invisible to the daytime traveler.

(7) Fuzziness

Now that you have tuned your mental vision to relationships, look again at the networks around you. If they still seem fuzzy, do not worry. Your relational glasses are not foggy, nor is your channel having technical difficulties. The boundaries of networks are often blurred and their activity often seems to turn on and off with no discernible regularity.

Think of your personal network. Can you clearly see who is in it and who is not? Is all of it always active with respect to you? Are your experiences with your friends always the same? If your networks are like our networks, the edges fade into an indistinct penumbra of relations and friends of friends. The personal network of Jack Eyerly, a "networker's networker" in Portland, Oregon (the "city of ash, roses and rain"), "is a scattergun of affectations and affections, a universe of layered maps and diagrams, dark and bright, illuminated one by the others."

Hierarchies and bureaucracies are clearly bounded. You are either in or out. You are either a part of the royal family or you are not. You either work for General Motors or you do not. Within these institutions, a major subsystem serves as a boundary, like the skin of a body or the borders of a nation. While some networks do indeed have limited, carefully defined memberships, and may even be closed to outside interactions, most networks are quite open and have a very loosely defined participantship. Network patterns ebb and flow according to the needs of the participants and consequences of external events.

In a note to us, Hine said that in her experience "no node in any network is aware of all the other nodes. It is the very nature of networks that they are fuzzily bounded if at all." Instead of being held together within a boundary, a network coheres from shared values, interests, goals, and objectives. A network is recognized by its clusters of interaction and channels of communication, rather than by a fixed boundary that includes and excludes.

It is shared values that establish the persisting identity of a network. Each person creates his or her own fuzzily bounded universe of interactions and values as members of many networks. For Eyerly, "From the beginning I knew the little knots I tied into the tapestry had resonance; they reverberate still. Each new tying is with more skill, but the original tingle remains the final value."

(8) Nodes and links

If you sat as a fly on our wall one day, you might have observed an exchange something like this:

> Robin in Toronto calls us in Boston. He wants to demonstrate the virtues of computer conferencing at his college; do we have any suggestions? We do. Call Barry at the University of Toronto. By the way, does Robin know of any networks in computer-aided art? He does. Robin suggests that we call Jackie at MIT in Cambridge or Ron in Los Angeles.

When we suggest that Robin call Barry, we are functioning as a link while treating Robin and Barry as nodes. When Robin suggests that we call Jackie and Ron, Robin is doing the linking and we are being a node.

In human networks, people are both nodes and links. It is people who set up relationships and it is people who are related. The roles are different but complementary, opposite but necessary for one another. As the above vignette illustrates, within one exchange a person may rapidly alternate between being a node and doing the linking.

Every participant of a network is potentially both a node and a link in the pattern of communication that constitutes the network as a whole. Each participant sometimes initiates or receives information as a node, and each participant sometimes acts as a link for other participants. At the level of personal networks, we daily experience this constant shifting back and forth between these two roles in communication.

In practice, in most established networks, some people and organizations will be nodes most of the time, while others will take on greater linking responsibilities. Indeed, the people we casually call "networkers" are the people who feel a personal calling to the task of setting up and maintaining relationships—links. Networks typically have a few participants who do most of the linking and many participants who are primarily nodes, but the possible combinations of these interrelationships are endless.

When modern physicists look at reality through their current models, they sometimes see a swarm of particles and they sometimes see a ripple of waves. Nodes and links are like particles and waves: networks may appear to be assemblies of nodes or webs of links, depending upon the perspective chosen. As nodes, participants in a network are like "particles," single entries in a mailing list or phone directory. People are just so many pieces of mail when you are licking stamps. In linking, however, participants seem more like "waves" of interaction, spectra of interests, and diffraction patterns of meaning. When you are talking on the telephone to one of those pieces of mail, the feeling is very different.

(9) Me and we

In every area of networking we reached in creating this book, we encountered a deep concern with the relationship between individual people and the many levels of social organization that seem to encompass the person.

With respect to people, networkers do not choose between the one and the many; they affirm both. Many networks express their vision as simultaneously encompassing the integrity and significance of the individual and concern with the importance of cooperation and collective interests. Like networks, people are holons, autonomous individuals inevitably connected to other people by a variety of relationships. We are each simultaneously "me" and "we."

In the prevailing scientific models of evolution, both old and new, the track of progress seems to run from atoms to cells to organisms to societies. The place of the human individual and the development of consciousness are completely finessed, skipped over

151

as if the question does not have its own unique meaning. On the one hand, people are seen as "special" organisms, and on the other hand people are regarded as simply units in societies. The implication of this viewpoint is that societies made up of people represent a more advanced stage of evolution than the individuals that compose them.

Recognizing a single track of evolution, we also perceive two interconnected rails on a spiraling track, like the double helix of DNA. One rail represents the successive development of more complex levels of individuality—amoebas to mollusks to apes to humans. The other rail represents the successive development of more complex levels of collectivity—mates to groups to tribes to civilizations. Our interpretation of evolution (see Chapter 10) is that the evolutionary development of individuals and their collective forms take place side by side.

Even without the framework of an evolutionary perspective, it is clear that in the worldview of the networkers of the Invisible Planet the value of the individual and the value of the group are equivalent. Of course, within the context of a particular issue, either individual rights or collective interests might be emphasized to redress larger imbalances. Concern may shift from pole to pole within one issue.

When networkers hold self-interest and group-interest together, these values often appear conflicting and ambiguous, perhaps paradoxical. Much of this discomfort naturally comes from our shared conceptual habit of dualism, which encourages us to choose one or the other pole of apparent opposites. But just as a physicist looks first at waves and then at particles to understand the one reality of both together, so each of us daily alternates between group and individual viewpoints to grasp the meaning of our one life.

A remarkable example of a network (and culture) that sees the unity in complements, rather than irreconcilable opposites, is expressed in the statement of principles by the National Indian Youth Council (NIYC):

NIYC views individuals as part of their community and there is no distinction between the two. While NIYC is concerned with individualistic problems such as economic poverty, employment discrimination, health care and education, the approach to these problems includes the community as a whole.

Within this worldview, individuals and communities grow and change together.

On the Invisible Planet, it is commonly recognized that social transformation cannot take place without personal transformation. Describing the common assumptions of the people in the Action Linkage network he has orchestrated, Theobald, for instance, says, "we accept that any effective pattern of action will require us to change both our personal values and the institutions which were formed in the industrial era." Expressing a similar understanding, the newsletter of the National Association for the Legal Support of Alternative Schools displays the following quotation from Kahlil Gibran (*The Prophet*) as a permanent feature of its masthead:

> If it is an unjust law you would abolish, that law was written with your own hand upon your own forehead. . . . And if it is a despot you would dethrone, see first that his throne erected within you is destroyed.

(10) Values

The context that gives coherence to a network is seen in values, not in objects. Network bonds tend to be subjective, rather than objective, more mental than physical, which is why, as we have said, networks seem so invisible to the object-trained eye.

Our human value heritage is deep and wide, rooted in the origin of the planet and life itself, blossoming over the past half billion years of births and deaths. With each new twist of evolution, life acquired new patterns of values to add to the values already established. The emergence of mortality and sex in simple cell groups, of instinct in reptiles and emotion in mammals, and of tools and speech in the far-distant human generations, have all contributed to our vast value heritage.

Strangely, among the values of the industrial age is the unfortunate paradox that human value is itself devalued. To the old-style scientific observer, measuring stick and rat cage in hand, values seemed mired in subjectivity. Values are "intangible" and cannot be registered on instrument dials; consequently, scientists have said, values must be "unreal." In contrast, among the values of the

networks of the Invisible Planet is the value of *valuing* itself.
Human values are considered "real" within the Invisible Planet,
and a concern with value is seen as essential for humane organization and purpose.

For members of the Southwest Research and Information Center,
"one of the most important characteristics of the Center is the
commitment of everyone connected with it." Networks cohere
through the shared commitment of their participants to a cluster
of values. Hine believes that the value bond is "perhaps the most
significant aspect of the segmentary mode of organization. . . . The
power of a unifying idea . . . lies in a deep commitment to a very
few basic tenets shared by all."

The values of the Invisible Planet do not present a consistent
tableau of step-by-step precepts for behavior. A set of values that
stresses collective interests over individual interests or the reverse
implies that more of one means less of the other. On the Invisible
Planet, a healthy dose of self-interest is regarded as acceptable if a
person also has a healthy measure of group-interest. Self-growth
is good when balanced with a consciousness of collective-growth.
The values of the Invisible Planet are about people and planet
together.

As we said at the outset of this book, it is not the network form
or process which distinguishes a movement for social change from
an elite breakfast club that runs an industry, nor is it bonds of
values. The difference between *all* networks and the *particular*
networks we selected to represent the Invisible Planet lies in the
values themselves.

Hine, Muller and others have pointed out that networks are now
most evident at the two extremes of power, but the ideologies in
these sectors are utterly different. Since the life of a network lies
in its values, then, says Hine:

> Perhaps one of the crucial tasks of the immediate future is to
> clarify and expose the underlying assumptions that provide
> the ideological "glue" for [networks] emerging at the various
> levels of the global social structure. The key to the future
> may very well be conceptual rather than organizational.

154

CHAPTER 10

Evolving networks

Most people have, at one moment or another in their lives, been led to the peak experience of asking the "big questions": Who are we? What are we doing here? Where are we going? Several millennia of recorded history indicate that these questions are eternal, questions that are addressed by every generation but ultimately and finally answered by none.

It is clear to many of us that now is a time when we must again collectively address the big questions and come up with viable means of meeting the awesome challenges and possibilities of the future. The hard work of acquiring a new "worldview," a new context of beliefs about what is real and what is possible, must be done by all of us in our own lives and work.

From our point of view, the most interesting and significant networks are those that manage to maintain an understanding of the larger context while coping with the minutiae of daily detail. For the Community Congress of San Diego, innovation is based on "caretaker" values, and it requires two abilities:

(1) An understanding of the "big picture", which [is] the ability to put suggestions or ideas into context or perspective—a world perspective, state perspective, local (county, city, neighborhood) perspective; and,

(2) An understanding of the very small, very specific operational details required to carry out a particular "big picture" or vision.

We have combined theory and practice, vision and detail, in our work and in our book. This book would have been impossible without countless hours of setting up files, skimming resources, writing letters, typing addresses, licking stamps, going to the post office, opening mail, and making innumerable small decisions. It also would have been impossible without a larger purpose and vision that guided our choices and led us through the many crises inevitable on any vision-quest. In the end, we could not have pulled together our voluminous and disparate universe of information about networks into a coherent whole without first articulating a theory and a vision that was at least satisfactory to ourselves.

Every person operates out of a mental framework of assumptions and images about the world even while going about the most ordinary of tasks. For most of us, most of the time, this worldview is not articulated.

Since the mental model that informs the networks of the Invisible Planet differs in some fundamental ways from the established worldview, networkers often consider it necessary to set up some theoretical underpinnings for their work and to explicitly state their essential values. Networkers vary, of course, in their predisposition to articulate theory, and there are many "natural networkers" with great intuitive resources who act effectively from inner wisdom without ever consciously creating a theory to explain what they are doing.

Summarizing the "big picture" is a tall order. Indeed, from the specialized point of view, it is an impossible order. Coincidentally, however, the same conceptual crises and influences that have led a few people to think about networks have led a few scientists to think about "general theory." There is an increasingly visible stream in modern science that flows out of the belief that the universe is both detailed and integrated, both infinitely diverse and richly patterned. This new stream has many contributing academic tributaries, from vaguely expressed "interdisciplinary interests" to clearly articulated approaches such as "general systems theory."

A "general" theory grows out of the recognition that many specialized theories may have something in common—perhaps a formula, or coefficient, or key concept. A general theory combines these similarities into a pattern and in doing so creates a transdisciplinary context for understanding the scientifically separated parts of the natural world. We believe that the tenets of general theory are precursors of a new philosophy about ourselves, our planet and our universe. The "new science" provides a "new metaphysics" for reconstructing our shared worldview.

General systems

Holism is a popular expression of the perennial philosophy that the details of the world are all related in broad patterns and encompassing contexts. While the legends of science abound with the search for universal laws and logic, for the most part the practice of science has focused on specific details about how the world works and the search for general patterns has been neglected. Over the past half century, however, a new approach has been developing within science that combines the traditional concern for analysis with a renewed interest in patterns.

In the years between the First and Second World Wars, various thinkers suggested that there are some universal principles common to all the sciences: in South Africa, Smuts propounded "holism"; in Russia, Bogdanov developed "*tektologia*" (the general science of organization); in England, Whyte put forth his "unitary principles"; and in Germany, Von Bertalanffy called his approach to unifying science "general systems theory."

In the late 1940s, the ideas of general theory started to coalesce, becoming a visible, permanent part of the scientific community in December 1954, when the Society for General Systems Research (SGSR) was founded, under the aegis of the American Association for the Advancement of Science (AAAS)—an event that occurred at the dawn of the Third Wave in Toffler's evolutionary chronology. While general systems ideas have yet to be absorbed into the scientific mainstream, it is interesting to note that the first president of SGSR, a quarter-century ago, Kenneth Boulding, was chairman of the board of AAAS in 1980.

The general systems idea is simple: it assumes that there are some organizational patterns common to all "systems," whether they be physical, biological, or human. Such patterns are inherent in the evolutionary process of the earth and humankind. A *system* may be generally defined as *a persisting identity of components and relationships*. Atoms, cells, organisms, people, nations, and galaxies are all examples of systems.

Using this definition, we can see that if everything with a patterned integrity is a system, then networks are systems. A *network* may be generally defined as *a persisting identity of nodes and links*. Examples of networks abound in this book. While saying that networks are a type of human organization, we can also say

157

that networks are a type of system. Our network model is a systems model. By defining a network as having a "persisting identity", we are saying that a network—a system—is a "whole" that encompasses a variety of "parts"—components and relationships. As we said in Chapter 9, holons, such as networks and people, represent two levels: the level of the whole and the level of the parts. Human bodies are wholes of interrelated organs. Nations are wholes of interrelated institutions. Atoms are wholes of interrelated particles. Networks are wholes of interrelated participants.

Virtually every general evolutionary theory that attempts to span the complete spectrum of systems—physical, biological and human—has described existence as a series of semiautonomous levels of organization. *Level* structure appears to be an inherent feature of all systems and thus of networks.

While most people are passingly familiar with the "building block" image of reality—atoms in cells in organisms in societies—people are less familiar with the idea that each level of a system maintains a substantial degree of autonomy within the context of larger systems. Governments, for example, are typically organized as national, regional, and local systems, each level being partially autonomous and partially dependent. Our city, Newton, functions both independently and interrelatedly within the Boston metropolitan area and the state of Massachusetts, which in turn functions in New England and as part of the United States of America. As citizens of Newton, Massachusetts, and the United States, we are also individuals who are autonomous yet dependent within families, which in turn are both autonomous and dependent within neighborhoods and communities. Every level is a holon.

The tension between autonomy and dependence is inherent in the idea of whole-part systems and networks. Since no system can be totally autonomous or totally dependent, forming and maintaining a "persisting identity" involves a dynamic balance between these two tendencies. The general name for this pattern of a balancing twosome is *complementarity*.

Complements are interrelated opposites. On the largest scale, evolution can be seen as a process of complementary tendencies to *order* and *disorder*. On the smallest scale, complementarity provides the explanatory vehicle for modern physics, the theory of quantum mechanics. In this model, reality is both *wave*-like and *particle*-like. Depending on your perspective, the "same" energy-matter may alternately appear as a wave and as a particle—a "now you see me, now you don't wavicle." Niels Bohr, the physicist who first propounded this model in the early decades of the twentieth century, later adopted a coat of arms bearing the Chinese yin/yang symbol of complementarity and the Latin inscription "*Contraria sunt complementa*" (Contraries are complements).

Life grows between the scales of the very large and the very small. Early life vibrated to the complements of light and dark, hot and cold, acidity and alkalinity, activity and passivity. Later life exploded in diversity with the emergence of the complements male and female, and birth and death. The human mind seems to harbor a complementary nature based on two brains in one, a right-hemisphere/left-hemisphere functioning. Human social life is a complex balance between the complements of individual freedom and collective responsibility.

Levels and *complements* are the two great interrelated metapatterns of systems theory. *Complementary* processes of order and disorder generate *levels* of evolutionary complexity, each *level* reflecting *complementary* dynamics of autonomy and dependence. The snake swallows its tail in a spiral of emergence.

Bringing these abstractions back into our own lives, we are a man and a woman who are unique individuals at the same time as we are a couple who depend upon one another for love and nurturance while also being parents who give to our children and receive love and affection in return. In short, we are complementary opposites (male and female) who by commitment and marriage have formed into a couple (another level, another complement of husband and wife) that functions to raise a family (yet another level, yet another complement as parents and children). The same is true for you in your relations with others.

We all know the everyday analytic rule of thumb for thinking about complex matters: to understand something, we are taught to break it down. The essence of the classical scientific method is that changing one thing at a time works best. In school, we were given one tool to use for probing the unknown: analysis. *Take the problem apart*: first disassemble, then study the parts, breaking the parts down if necessary, and, finally, reassemble. In practice, the strategy is a good one for a car, and a poor one for a cat. While you can take a functioning car apart piece by piece and then put it back together again and drive away, you cannot do the same thing to a cat: once disassembled, a cat will never purr again. Some things respond well to analysis; other things do not.

In a similar way, the old paradigm habitually pits opposites against one another, considering them "irreconcilable" and "contradictory." Matter is real and mind is not. Males are better than females. Disorder is the one universal one-way tendency. Objective is good, subjective is not. Black or white. The combinations are endless.

It is important to recognize that duals and opposites are as bound up in Western philosophy and culture as they are in the East. In the industrial West, however, the rule of thumb is that where there are two, one prevails. One is right, two is a disagreement.

In duals (and duels), one wins; in complements (and compliments), both dance.

New paradigms are supposed to subsume the old ones. Obviously, the "dominant-submissive" interpretation of opposites can be accommodated within the framework of complementarity, since paired opposites can take on a variety of balanced and unbalanced forms: sex roles, for example, can be male-dominated, female-dominated, rigorously equal, or flexibly supportive. Similarly, traditional analysis, "breaking down," can certainly be done within the framework of levels simply by continually focusing on "lower" or "smaller" levels and ignoring "higher" or "larger" levels. Analysis and dualism are not "wrong", just limited.

Levels and complements can be useful abstractions, helping to translate experience into the new paradigm and serving as handy conceptual "rules of thumb." *Levels* and *complements* are conceptual tools that subsume and extend the old paradigm tools of *analysis* and *dualism*. As a rule of thumb, *levels* means looking at wholes as well as parts, seeing ever-more-encompassing contexts as well as seeing ever smaller pieces. As a rule of thumb, *complementarity* means looking at process as well as structure, of seeing interplay between contrasting tendencies as well as dominant trends of the moment.

When you are stuck at one level, look for an answer at another level; when you see one process, look for the "hidden face," the complementary process.

General network theory

Efforts to understand networks benefit greatly from the general systems perspective and collectively may be considered a species of systems theory. So well does the concept of a network capture the essence of a system that, for some purposes, "network" may be a better vehicle to describe general phenomena than "system."

The essence of a network can be expressed in terms of just two characteristics, holons and values:

(1a') A network is a set of free-standing participants cohering through shared interests and values.

Participants may be individual, groups, or nations, but it is the essential autonomy of the composing parts that identifies the network pattern of organization.

"Network" is a word brought into the domain of social entities because of its strong, clear metaphorical roots. A need to describe a value-based, spread-out, process-oriented, multicentered social form was spontaneously met by the word network and its associations from fishing nets to telephone nets. Its use as a clarifying concept has just begun to be tapped.

Our "public" definition of a social network (1a above) is actually a special case of a more general definition. A computer network, for example, is composed of free-standing computers cooperating through shared protocols. Or, more generally:

(1b) A network is a system of semi-autonomous subsystems cohering through shared qualities.

In a formal definition, it is important to emphasize the *semi*-autonomy of a network part, for no entity that we know of is totally self-sufficient. Every entity in the universe is part of a more inclusive entity, and is itself composed of semi-autonomous subsystems. This is the *holon*omic nutshell of the systems perspective.

Now in its second quarter-century, systems theory has progressed from the Leibnizian dream of a "universal calculus" to a dynamic discipline drawing resources from both mathematical and intuitive sources. Anatole Rapoport, a mathematician and psychologist who was a Society for General Systems Research founder, often described general systems theory (GST) as a meeting ground for "hard" and "soft" science.

"Hard" science is about "hard" systems. "Hard" systems are those that can be mathematically modeled, which, writes Rapoport, unfortunately apply to a relatively limited class of systems. Rapoport's more inclusive, "soft" definition of a system is:

(2a) "A system is a portion of the world that is perceived as a unit and that is able to maintain its 'identity' in spite of changes going on in it."

In Rapoport's view, his definition covers both material systems and nonmaterial systems, like languages. It is easy to see networks of all types meeting this definition, whether physical networks, social networks, or abstract networks. Look closely, however:

(2b) A network is a portion of the world that is perceived as a whole and is able to maintain an identity in spite of the changing identities in it.

Bringing the network holon aspect into this definition has sharpened the perception of complex whole parts making up the inclusive network whole. A network is not made up of a dependent collection of parts with no meaning in themselves. A network is made up of parts that themselves have identities.

(3a) A system is a whole of interacting parts.

(3b) A network is a whole of interacting parts with whole identities.

While a general definition of general phenomena can use either "system" or "network" as the entity, the network perspective brings parts into a complementary balance with wholes. This provides powerful conceptual leverage when applying systems principles to the perennial problem of the human sciences: how to distinguish what is important in the buzzing, booming, confusion. What a network perspective suggests is this: look inside for the semi-autonomous parts, the interactions that compose the whole; and look outside to a greater whole of which this whole is a part.

GST and GNT

Kenneth Boulding, SGSR's first president, once characterized GST as "not so much a body of doctrine as it is a point of view or even an intellectual value orientation. . . ." It is in the broadest meaning of systems theory that the network concept might have the most to offer.

Networking seems to attract people who strive to combine the practical and the theoretical. For the past fifteen years, Anthony J. N. Judge has been in the Brussels office of the Union of International Associations (UIA) composing network theory alongside his compilation of international networks. A remarkable companion volume of the UIA directory series, the *Yearbook of World Problems and Human Potential* (1976, 1985), brings together both abstract and concrete networks of organizations, problems and concepts. In the 1976 appendix, Judge writes:

> A fundamental difficulty today is the predilection for simplistic hierarchical representation of the interrelationships between concepts, between organizations, and between problems. This is so despite the constant exposure to the evidence that these hierarchies do not contain the complexity with which society has to deal. . . . Neither a hierarchical organization nor a hierarchy of concepts can handle a network of environmental problems, for example, without leaving many dangerous gaps through which unforeseen problems may emerge and be uncontainable.

From the earliest days of GST, systems taxonomists have endeavored to sketch outlines of how everything is included and related to everything else. Such efforts and the methodologies that followed were quite successful with concrete things but less satisfactory with respect to abstract entities. While abstraction—relational reality—was acknowledged, the main stream of systems theory has stuck with the concrete. James G. Miller provides an excellent example in *Living Systems*, arguing that while abstract entities like a "presidency" may be real, as a practical matter it is easier to study a concrete "president." He commented that when scientists deal with abstracted systems, they "easily forget the intrasystem relationships in concrete systems."

The term "network" seems to have been naturally adopted precisely to describe the fuzzy, complex, relationally rich associations like brains, languages, personal behavior and social groups that "system" is so poor in illuminating. Connotations of structure, control and predictability accompany the system concept, qualities important, of course, to the understanding of many concrete, physical entities. However, the network concept represents dynamic processes, loose structure, and unpredictable entities, viewpoints essential for understanding abstract and human realities. What the network concept seems to do well is provide a context for perceiving both intra- and intersystemic relationships of recognizable wholes and parts in both abstract and concrete phenomena.

"General network theory" (GNT) arises out of the recognition that "network" can meaningfully replace "system" in all nonmathematical GST formalisms without loss of generality. Using the notion of network in abstract and human domains is extending systems insights to these crucial intellectual areas.

GNT is not proposed as a replacement for GST, but rather as a complement. As Judge wrote in a prescient paper entitled "System-network complementarity," "Rather than attempt to resolve the distinction between system and network, it may be useful to conceive of the two terms as being different but complementary conceptual approaches to a structure-process continuum."

Networking, secret is buried in the verb. While networks represent structures as do systems, there is no "systeming" like "networking." The active "to network" has accompanied the development of social networks. In networking, people recognize the essential reality of relationships, of perceptions, of information flow. Networks and networking captures process in a metaphor cross-hatched with structure.

Convening an information philosophy

As Robert Muller says, "What is really needed today is a new philosophy of life within our global conditions, a new hope, a new vision of the future . . . not . . . the product of any one person, but . . . a collective product" (see Chapter 8).

By the end of this millenium, a global information philosophy will have coalesced. With roots at the start of the century, this worldview will include the ideas we so seem to need and cherish—global and human—while also being scientific and philosophic.

Early in this century, Einstein and the "Copenhagen Group" of physicists offered the first glimpse of successful nonmechanistic scientific models. In the 1920s and 1930s, theoretical biology shook off its reductionist limits and began to view whole cells, organisms and environments. Through the 1940s, cybernetic and information pioneers laid the theoretical foundations for the technological explosion to come. New concepts of "information" passed through the materialistic paradigm without stopping.

In 1945, humanity crossed a threshold.

In a six-month period, three events announced the irrevocable coming of a new world, for better and for worse. In June, the charter of the United Nations was ratified; in August, the atomic bomb was dropped on Hiroshima and Nagasaki; in December, ENIAC, the first electronic computer, completed its tests. Each of these events had antecedents, precursors and a history, but each presaged a fundamental change in human experience. The biophysicist John Platt points to 1945 as Year 0.

With the dawn of the 1960s, developing hot spots of change in the Western world burst into the social sphere. In the US, civil rights opened the floodgates of social activism. Vietnam came and went. The women's movement and ecology came and stayed. Social movements transformed into personal explorations. Explorations and movements spawned networks.

Now, in the 1980s, as we look to the last decade of the millennium, we see the emergent events of forty years ago clearly shaping our daily present. A global economy and society, linked by information technologies, is poised to flower, yet it may instantly perish.

Shifting worldviews

The structure of the emergent society is the network.

Virginia Hine's 1977 four-page cornerstone in the foundation of information philosophy begins: "[In] piecing together a range of observations by anthropologists, sociologists, economists, and political scientists, [it seems] that the basic paradigm of a future socio-cultural system is already born—muling and puking in its infantile state, but here."

In the posthumously published sequel to her classic essay ("How do we get from here to there?"), Hine related the rise of networks to a concomitant change in the sieve of concepts through which we filter the world. "A shift in the *structural paradigm*—the basic pattern of social organization and institutions"—is occurring with "a shift in the *conceptual paradigm*, the cultural world view, the framework of thought, a shared set of basic assumptions," she wrote.

While the "new age" predictions of "transformation" and "paradigm shifts" have gone out of style, the recognition that we on

165

planet Earth are undergoing *some* rapid (r)evolutionary change is now a regular feature of Sunday supplements.

For most of us, the 1980s recognition of undeniable change is composed in concrete technological and economic images. As the microchip blinks and chirps its way into everyone's life, common experience of work and play shift into the fast lane of change in the still-embryonic information economy. Change from "industry" to "information" clearly affects the nature of work, and surely affects the home and play conditions surrounding work.

Accepting the concrete evidence of an "information age" provides a model for perceiving a network of related large-scale changes. The driving dynamic of escalating computing power and plunging computer costs paves the paths of change across society. New social forms, different from the bureaucratic box chart mass-produced by industrialism, are aborning.

Networks are now "new" because the information age is providing a ripe environment for their nurture. And extinction. Astonishingly various and notoriously fragile, today's social networks are in that part of the evolutionary spurt that requires experimentation. Standards and models are still in the making.

At the same time, networks are very old, as sociological historians attest. The small-group network was likely the original human organization, and has probably played a background role ever since.

Like organisms, organizations evolve. Consider the "emergence" of mammals as a metaphor for what is happening now with networks: mammals existed for millions of years as a backwater evolutionary branch before their moment came. "Suddenly" they exploded in diversity and numbers after the precipitous decline of the reptile family and drastic changes in global climate. While it might be a bit harsh to liken bureaucracies to reptiles (though it's not uncommon to hear them referred to as dinosaurs) and perhaps premature to equate the greenhouse effect to drastic climate changes, the evolutionary analogies for the development of human organizations can be instructive.

Yoneji Masuda, writing for the past three decades on the rise of "the information society" with the development and spread of computers, begins his book *The Information Society as Post-Industrial Society* with a quote from Nobel Prize winner Herbert Simon, the pioneer information theorist: "In recorded history there have perhaps been three pulses of change powerful enough to alter [humans] in basic ways. The introduction of agriculture. . . . The Industrial Revolution . . . [and] the revolution in information processing technology. . . ." Instrumental in Japanese government planning for the present and future information society, Masuda sees the network form as basic to both the electronic and social expressions of change.

Information reality

As environment and behavior change, so does the mind. As technology shifts from heavy metal to light silicon and burdensome bureaucracies break up into nebulous networks, so do conceptual filters change. In our mind's eye, we shift from seeing discrete autonomous dismantleable things to understanding increasingly complex, inextricably entwined relationships.

This is truly how it is for people using computers—which is perhaps why so many users experience such mental anguish. One example is this: you work all day on something, then in a stupid moment of forgetfulness, nothing more than a single keystroke, you destroy all you have done. In the modern experience of computing, the mind is stretched to keep track of dozens of simultaneous interactive considerations, none of which can be "seen" in any literal sense.

Computers are clearly affecting bedrock perceptions of reality. The complementary interaction of space and time, long an abstraction of theoretical physicists, is the daily experience of the computer user, juggling processing time with memory space before dinnertime. Asynchronous computer-mediated conversations across continents and time zones leave participants with a curious *déjà vu* sense of the ordinary and extraordinary as new patterns of social interaction rapidly coalesce and disintegrate. Like a mail "experience" of a letter from someone in Texas arriving on top of one from the person in Colorado who mentioned the Texan to you, electronic synchronicities also occur, and temper our adventure with time— J & J's morning in Boston being Kerstin's evening in Sweden, and Peter's next day in Australia.

In its essence, information reality differs from material reality. Matter, when used, is used up. Information, when used, adds up.

Ontology, esoteric ruminations on the nature of reality, now has literal, practical implications for everyday life. It is *ontological* differences between matter and information that lie behind the unfolding industrial/information shift.

Industrialism is based on transformations of matter. Entropy, the inevitable decline and decay of matter, ensures an economics of scarcity. A still not fully understood economics of abundance is based on transformations of information. This economics copes with overload and copying, the problems of multiplication rather than substraction.

Industrialism came with an ontology that declared matter to be the basic and only constituent of reality. Information comes with its own ontological bias—to relations. New paradigms, however, do not necessarily destroy their antecedents; they may include them. To spin an information reality of complex weaves of ephemeral connections, we still need a loom of the hard knocks-on-the-table material reality.

In the information paradigm, matter and relations are complements, both part of reality.

Philosophy follows practice in the information era. Information philosophy, what little there is of it, has been pragmatic stuff leaving us with new daily words like feedback. Cybernetic principles survive because they so obviously work in the electronic world. Networks arise in multinational companies and urban neighborhoods because they meet people's needs. An information economy is becoming dominant in America and Japan because that is where new wealth is being created.

Though in the background, the new information philosophy can already be seen in outline. In classical philosophical categories, it has an ontology of relations, an epistemology of levels and complements, and an ethics based on the reality of value.

These features of an information worldview were already present two decades ago when Kenneth Boulding wrote *The Meaning of the Twentieth Century*, a prophetic anticipation of the current industry/information shift. In his conclusion, "A strategy for the transition," Boulding describes the network of thinkers and doers fashioning the new paradigm:

There is in the world today an "invisible college" of people in many different countries and many different cultures, who have this vision of the nature of the transition through which we are passing and who are determined to devote their lives to contributing towards its successful fulfillment. Membership in this college is consistent with many different philosophical, religious, and political positions. It is a college without a founder and without a president, without buildings and without organization.

This college remains invisible, but has swollen by millions of people in networks around the world who are engaged in changing themselves and the world. The college convenes in many places simultaneously. Its seminars are held in storefront offices and penthouse suites, continuing through the mail, on the telephone, and online. Leadership is fluid and hard to spot. Distinctions between teachers and taught are blurry. Curricula are under perpetual revision.

Times are tough. Everyone seems to be talking about the delicate balance between hope and despair. If we're too hopeful, we're unrealistic, failing to confront the magnitude of our problems. If we're too despairing, we're paralyzed, immobilized by the overwhelming impossibility of being able to change anything. But remember! Ours is a time of transition. Lessons from evolution are becoming part of human history.

Transformation

One idea in the new worldview is "transformation". Transformation means radical, fundamental change, usually occurring suddenly and out of chaos. The idea is not abstract. It is of the essence of our time.

In 1948, the English philosopher/physicist/banker Lancelot Law Whyte published *The Next Development in Man*, written during the years 1941–43, while he was immersed in the fire and rubble of war among the great industrial-scientific nations of the world. As part of the team developing the first jet for the Allies, Whyte was thoroughly involved in the war effort. Even so, Whyte was also peering through a new scientific lens of general theory, seeing the indicators of a great transformation in the development of the human species.

To think effectively about the plausibility and significance of a major evolutionary change in our time, a long view of the whole of human evolution is required. Whyte saw first important transformations in human history, beginning with the primordial transition of primate biology to symbolic consciousness and continuing to the now-occurring transition from the industrial European age to an age of global unity.

(1) *Circa 5–2 million BC* With an indistinct ancestry at least 2 million and perhaps 5 million years old, nomadic, hunter-gatherer "hominids" gradually developed the skills of symbol making, tool making, fire use, and speech. These hominids were the primate precursors of the modern human subspecies, *Homosapiens* sapiens, who appeared around 40,000 BC.

(2) *Circa 10,000 BC* Suddenly, where bands of twenty had roamed, settled agricultural communities of 200 now appeared, marking a shift that is often considered to be the ancient dawn of civilization. Within a millennium, agriculture had sprouted, flowered, and taken root, and religious tombs and temples multiplied, "inventions" that were to become the central pillars of the ancient era. By 5000 BC neolithic towns had grown to cities of 10,000 and the great theocracies of Egypt and Mesopotamia had started their ascent to splendor. Under stress resulting from multiple influences such as intercultural trade, the adoption of writing, savage war, and geological catastrophes, the towering but fragile hierarchies of ancient gods and priestly rulers began to disintegrate in the last two millennia BC.

(3) *Circa 600 BC* Out of the confusion of multiple deities, a new voice in human consciousness emerged, an early self-conscious rationalism that was archetypified in the Golden Age of Greek thought, beginning with the Athenian lawmaker Solon and culminating in the twin wellsprings of Western worldviews, Plato and Aristotle. Often recognized as the dawn of Western civilization, this period is also the era of Gautama Siddhartha (Buddha), Lao-tse (the founder of Taoism), and Confucius (Kung Fu-tse), who represent a similar transition in the East.

(4) *Circa AD 1600* Modern history begins with the shift to the scientific-industrial worldview, which developed out of the monastic ponderings of Bacon, the movable type of Gutenberg, the astrological reveries of Kepler, the telescope of Galileo, and the absolutes of Newton. This set of ideas, which reached its

170

peak of certainty and influence at the end of the nineteenth century, still dominates the thinking of modern society.

(5) *Circa AD 1920–2000* The signs of the next great transformation in human development first became visible in the years following World War I. Predicting that the many threads of change would rapidly coalesce into a coherent worldview in the post-World War II years, Whyte said that this transition would probably be complete by the end of the twentieth century. Or else, he felt, humankind would be in serious trouble.

In 1964, Kenneth Boulding, one of the first scientists to recognize the potential applicability of general systems theory, published *The Meaning of the Twentieth Century*. In this little book, Boulding proposed that within the broad sweep of human evolution two really important transitions are apparent: one happened roughly 12,000 years ago and the other is happening now. Boulding sees all human history, from the agricultural dawn of civilization to the beginning of the twentieth century, as one huge epoch—that he calls simply "civilization," and that he sees as coming after several million years of "precivilization" hunting and gathering. The "meaning of the twentieth century" is that *now* is the time of a second great transition in human evolution—to what Boulding calls "postcivilization."

In 1980, the futurist Alvin Toffler published *The Third Wave*, a best-seller, which interprets human history in terms of three "waves of development." The First Wave on Toffler's calendar, which he characterizes as agricultural, begins after the earliest precivilization era and spans the period from 10,000 BC to the emergence of science in the sixteenth and seventeenth centuries AD. The Second Wave, which he characterizes as industrial, is the worldview that dominated the globe until around 1955. For the past three decades, Toffler says, we have been hurtling into the future on the crest of a great Third Wave of human evolution.

Perhaps the most apocalyptic example of this viewpoint is the widely quoted remark by the biophysicist John Platt, who wrote, "The present generation is the hinge of history. . . . We may now be in the time of the most rapid change in the whole evolution of the human race, either past or to come."

Although they differ on the stages of human evolution, these writers have a common theme: we live in an evolutionarily significant moment, a period of confusion and instability that nevertheless carries the seeds for the emergence of the next level of human development, both personal and social.

Emergent evolution

Where do networks fit in on this scale? We believe that networking—people making connections between people—is as old as the first symbol-making hominids and has survived and changed over the several million years of crucial transitions in human development. Networks of tool makers, fire starters, cave painters, mammoth hunters, and sign speakers must have organized into various social support systems to cope with personal and collective survival during the first millions of years of human existence. Informal networks were undoubtedly important in the era of ancient civilization, dominated by the development of elaborate control hierarchies, when, for example, those rejecting the prevailing authority, such as the early Jews and Christians, survived and grew on the branches of their network tree.

Networks have certainly been important during the industrial-rational age. Operating within bureaucracies, this period's characteristic organizational form, is the so-called "old-boy network," a term that belies the real influence and power such a peer group holds. While informal networks of people with a common worldview have performed a crucial integrating function for established institutions, networks also have been the foundation for revolutions in this era—from the Committees of Correspondence of the American Revolution to the Spanish anarchists to the cells of the classical communist revolution to the many contemporary media voices and congregations of single-issue movements.

The idea of transformation on the largest scale is based on a radically revised view of evolution—a very charged word at the end of the twentieth century, as evidenced by a 1981 US court battle over what children should be taught about the origin of life. Unnoticed in the current political confusion surrounding the debate of "creationists" versus "neo-Darwinians" is a growing scientific underground that is merging Darwin's evolutionary theory into a new, more comprehensive model that is sometimes called *emergent evolution*. Emergent evolution is a simple term encompassing the

many converging ideas of the past quarter century of anthropologists such as Gregory Bateson, biologists such as Ludwig von
Bertalanffy, philosophers such as Lancelot Law Whyte, economists
such as Kenneth Boulding, psychologists such as Abraham Maslow,
and humanists such as Arthur Koestler.

Four ideas in the new paradigm of evolution are important to
us in understanding contemporary change networks: emergence,
inclusion, transition and acceleration. The principle of *emergence*
suggests that there are some qualities in networks that are clearly
new in human history. The principle of *inclusion* suggests that
earlier forms of human organization are carried into future forms.
The principle of *transition* (including both periods of "chaos" and
moments when the process seems to "step-back-to-leap-forward")
explains the current period of confusion and also suggests that new
networks are reaching back to earlier stages of human evolution
in order to fashion a synthesis for the future. Finally, from our
present vantage point in time, it appears that terrestrial evolution
is a process of progressive *acceleration*. Each cycle of stability and
transformation leading to a new level of organization is shorter
than the cycle that went before—which explains why momentous
evolutionary change is possible in our time.

(1) Emergence

For millions of years, hominids existed without fire. Then, suddenly
(in terms of paleo-archaeological time scales), they discovered how
to use and conserve fire. In evolutionary theory, this idea is called
emergence, referring to the notion that evolution seems to proceed
through cycles of long, slow swells of "horizontal" change followed
by wind-whipped chops of rapid "vertical" change. This pattern
is sometimes represented as a series of "steps," like a set of stairs,
up a scale of progressive development. But the steps of evolution
do not always march steadily up the slope of progress. Rather,
they appear to zigzag their way toward greater complexity, with
evolution sometimes appearing to be retreating, rather than
advancing.

The Darwinian-industrial concept of evolution portrays a
process of sluggish continual change: from slime to slug to reptile
to ape to human. According to the conventional model, isolated,
random mutations, which are recorded as genetic variations, have

survived a natural competitive struggle (the survival of the fittest), slowly building up terrestrial complexity to human life—layer by sedimentary layer.

While natural selection is certainly a powerful process in evolution, the new paradigm of emergent evolution also recognizes another process, transformation, in which sudden and sharp discontinuities punctuate the progress of slow change. These rifts either signal a leap to a new, more complex level of life or they signal a devastating crash to some earlier level of life. Over the long haul, human life and civilization are testimony to the fact that, so far, life on this planet appears to have leaped more often than collapsed. The theory of emergence suggests that evolution does indeed generate "new things under the sun," that there is a creative principle of order operating together with the randomizing principle of disorder. There is a process of building up as well as a process of tearing down.

In the longest view, there have been two fundamental, sharp transformations in life on earth: between purely *physical* systems (such as atoms, minerals and clocks) and *biological* forms (such as amoebas, reptiles and rats); and between purely *biological* life and *human* life (such as us and you). The biologist Theodosius Dobzhansky has called these transitions the "quantum leaps" of evolution and the "points of evolutionary transcendence." An amoeba is as different from a rock as a person is from a dog.

Each of these major levels—physical, biological and human—contains clearly identifiable levels of organization. Quarks, subatomic particles, atoms and molecules are successive levels of physical organization; cells, organelles, organs and organisms are levels of biological organization. What Whyte, Boulding, Toffler and others are trying to perceive are the significant transitions that mark the evolutionary development of *humankind*, the levels and periods of emergent transformation in human psyches and societies.

(2) Inclusion

The theory of emergent evolution provides a context for understanding networking as both an extremely old and an entirely new human activity. Emergent evolution describes a process of long, slow change alternating with short, rapid change and sudden transformation. As a cumulative process, earlier levels of life are absorbed into later levels of life. In biological development, for example, the cell could not have coalesced without stable molecular structures; organs could not have arisen without pre-existing cells; and complex organisms could not have appeared without the existence of specialized functions. Smaller worlds are subsumed into wider worlds.

Within the human world, we can see this process of successive inclusion at work in communications. The invention of the press on which this book is printed was only possible because writing was developed 3000 years before, itself an impossible invention had not the first spoken words been uttered several million years earlier. The telephone, television and the computer all stand on the shoulders of speaking, writing and printing, at the same time as these electromagnetic media possess qualities of speed, distribution and flexibility that are entirely new in human experience. The concept of the computer includes the first symbol ever conceived and the first word ever spoken by our most distant human ancestors.

(3) Transition

In his now-classic essay *The Structure of Scientific Revolutions*, Thomas Kuhn brilliantly described the chaos that exists just prior to and during periods of transition between "old" and "new" scientific worldviews, a recurrent pattern in the evolution of scientific thought. Dominant scientific models reach a certain peak of success in being able "to explain everything" just when anomalies—odd fragments of experiments and theories that do not fit the prevailing view—become numerous and troublesome. Adherents of new viewpoints—generally younger, uncommitted scientists—attack the dominant model and promote a profusion of alternative models.

A "clash of worldviews" between scientific perspectives creates a period of confusion and tension that is suddenly resolved by the presentation of a new synthesis. The new paradigm invariably incorporates the now-apparent partial truths of the older model, provides consistent explanations for the precipitating anomalies, and opens up new territory for scientific exploration. In time, the "new synthesis" becomes the "established model" and begins to reach its exploratory limits, as a new cycle of challenge, chaos and transformation ensues.

While many modern theorists have recognized that "chaos-in-transformation" is a natural part of the evolutionary pattern, some have gone farther and perceived that in major transitions there is also a distinct "step-back-to-leap forward." Kuhn, for example, suggests that new paradigms emerge not from established, successful, "mature" scientists but rather from newcomers who are "embryonic" scientists not locked into the old structure—like the young Swiss patent clerk Albert Einstein. What Kuhn and others have suggested is that when evolution gets "stuck" at a certain level of organization, it may revert to an earlier, more plastic level of order before the leap to a new synthesis is possible. This back-and-forth pattern also contributes to evolution's "zigzag" appearance. In our culture, the idea is encapsulated in the expression "one step back and two steps forward."

The author and systems theorist Arthur Koestler, who used the French expression *"reculer pour mieux sauter"* to describe this pattern, has drawn a parallel between biological change and the process of human creativity in science, art and humor. Koestler suggests that when a creative person has become consciously stuck on a problem, his/her mind retreats first to a lower level of consciousness in order to find the pathway to a creative solution. Below the level of full wakefulness, previously unrecognized associations crystallize, exploding in a sudden synthesis—a flash of insight. In a moment, the mind leaps over the problem to the solution, from the stuck place to a new level of understanding. Referring to the subtle part the unconscious plays in scientific creativity, one physicist cracked that all great discoveries are a product of the "three B's": insights come while in Bed, in the Bath, or while waiting for a Bus.

John Platt believes a new international order is developing in the retreat-to-advance pattern. We are stuck, he contends, at the nation-state level of human organization. World order is not emerging from alliances of nations, which are notoriously fragile and incomplete. Rather, he says, thousands of subnational organizations are forming multinational associations and creating an increasingly interdependent web of international corporate, institutional, and professional relationships that are not directly dependent on national governments. That is, we are not moving directly from national to international government but, rather, are detouring through earlier subnational stages in order to re-form at a higher transnational level.

(4) Acceleration

A popular view of evolution's vast time span is dramatized by Carl Sagan's use of a one-year calendar to represent the significant dates in cosmic-terrestrial development. Sagan's calendar begins with the Big Bang birth of the universe on 1 January, shows the formation of the earth on 14 September, the dinosaurs reigning around Christmas, and the first humans appearing on the last day, 31 December. In the last minute of this last day, 11:59:20 p.m., to be precise, agriculture emerged along with gods and priests. All the rest of human history occupies only the last few seconds of this cosmic calendar.

Seeing human history as but a flash in the cosmic drama and the human home as but a mote in the vastness of the universe certainly rids us of our bloated sense of anthropocentric self-importance. Yet, minuteness also robs us of a sense of significance, the sense that we play some role in the drama that has meaning for the largest whole. Viewing the vastness of cosmic time, it is difficult to imagine significant evolutionary shifts happening in our lifetime—the equivalent of fractions of a second on the scale of Sagan's calendar. Transformation over a few generations is understandable only when the accelerating pace of evolution is recognized. A quick review of "the big picture" illustrates this idea.

Life first appeared on earth a billion or so years after the planet's birth almost 5 billion years ago. The bacteria-based bioplanet developed slowly for more than 3 billion years (!) until life exploded in diversity with the coemergence of sex (male and female) and mortality (birth and death) 500 million years ago. Mammals became numerous 75 million years ago. Erect, tool-making primates appeared between 2 and 5 million years ago. Humans settled towns 12,000 years ago. The "ancient" cultures of Greece and Rome flourished 2500 years ago. The industrial era is less than 400 years old.

Galactic change is measured in billions and millions of years, biological change in millions and hundreds of thousands of years, and distant human change in thousands and hundreds of years.

Billions, millions, millennia, centuries—today, change of evolutionary significance is measured in decades and years.

Textbook Darwinian theory portrays evolution as slow moving and incremental—a process that "takes a long time." Within that worldview it is difficult to imagine that evolution is accelerating, apt to suddenly shift direction, and may indeed be recognizable within the span of a single human life. Yet, through the mental lens of the new paradigm, our responsibility, right now, for the evolution of ourselves and the planet is inescapable.

We can only wonder how long it will be before evolutionary changes will seem to approach "light speed," the recognition that it is the moments of spontaneous human creativity which are the pulsing tip of the evolutionary process unfolding on the terrestrial stage. Even when human history is seen as a flicker and flash in time, it is the *last* and *next* flash of earth's evolution, and it inherits the significance of all the earlier flashes.

The future

"The future" is not something that will "happen" to us. We make the future every moment we live, an ancient idea that is the very essence of "karma" and most readily understood in the West through the biblical passage "As you sow, so shall you reap."

Our future is born out of our transforming ideas, out of our original and most basic human attribute, which is the ability to create images of a world that has not yet existed, but may.

May there be peace on earth—all else follows.

Network directory

This directory provides contact information for the organizations mentioned in the text of *The Networking Book*. We maintain the directory as one of the services of The Networking Institute, P.O. Box 66, West Newton, Massachusetts, USA, 617/891–4727.

Action Linkage, 153 Jefferson Street, Box 2240, Wickenburg, AZ 85358.
American Association for the Advancement of Science, 1333 H. Street, NW, Washington, DC 20005.
American Humanist Association, P.O. Box 146, 7 Harwood Drive, Amherst, NY 14226.
Anvil Press, P.O. Box 37, Millville, MN 55957.
Arthur D. Little, Inc., 25 Acorn Park, Cambridge, MA 02140.
Association for Experiential Education, University of Colorado, P.O. Box 249, Boulder, CO 80309.
Association for Humanistic Psychology, 325 Ninth Street, San Francisco, CA 94103.
B'nai Or, 6723 Emlen Street, Philadelphia, PA 19119.
Boston Women's Health Book Collective, P.O. Box 192, West Somerville, MA 02144.
Buckminster Fuller Institute, 1743 South La Cienega Blvd., Los Angeles, CA 90035.
Coalition for Alternatives in Postsecondary Education, c/o Council on Higher Education, 1050 US Route 127 South, West Frankfort Office Complex, Frankfort, KY 40601.
Community Congress of San Diego, 3052 Clairmont Drive, San Diego, CA 92117.
CompuServe, 5000 Arlington Centre Boulevard, Columbus, OH 43220.
Council for the Advancement of Experiential Learning, Suite 203, 10840 Little Patuxent Parkway, Columbia, MD 21044.
Cultural Exchange Service, 240 East Limberlost, Tucson, AZ 85705.
Digital Equipment Corporation, Distributed Systems, 146 Main Street, Maynard, MA 01754.
Displaced Homemakers Network, Suite 817, 1010 Vermont Avenue, NW, Washington, DC 20005.

Electronic Information Exchange System, New Jersey Institute of
Technology, 323 High Street, Newark, NJ 07102.

Environmental Action Foundation, 1525 New Hampshire Avenue, NW,
Washington, DC 20036.

Environmental Research Laboratory, Tucson International Airport, 7250
S. Tucson Blvd., Tucson, AZ 85706.

Esalen Institute, Big Sur, CA 93920.

Experiment in International Living, Institutional Relations, Kipling
Road, Brattleboro, VT 05301.

Farallones Institute, 15290 Coleman Valley Road, Occidental, CA
95465.

Friends of Peace Pilgrim, 43480 Cedar Avenue, Hemet, CA 92344.

Friends of the Earth, 1045 Sansome Street, San Francisco, CA 94111.

Greenpeace USA, 139 Main Street, Cambridge, MA 02142.

Groupware Systems, 695 Fifth Street, Lake Oswego, OR 97034.

Hanuman Foundation Tape Library, P.O. Box 61498, Santa Cruz, CA
95061.

Health Promotion Directorate, National Health and Welfare, Guy
Fevreau Complex, East Tower, 200 Dorchester Blvd., Montreal,
Quebec, H2Z 1X4, Canada.

Insight Meditation Center, Pleasant Street, Barre, MA 01005.

Institute for the Information Society, Fujimara Building, 2–15–29,
Shinjuku, Shinjuku-ku, Tokyo, Japan.

International Commons, Inc., 296 Newton Street, Suite 350, Waltham,
MA, 02154.

International Network for Social Network Analysis, 455 Spadina Ave.,
4th Fl., Toronto, Ontario, M5S 2G8, Canada.

Invisible College of Robert A. Smith, III, 205 Briarhill Road, Abbeville,
AL 36310.

J. C. Penney Company, Inc., Forum, 1301 Avenue of the Americas, New
York, NY 10019.

Learning Resources Network, 1221 Thurston, Manhattan, KS 66502.

Lorian Association, P.O. Box 663, Issaquah, WA 98027.

Massachusetts Corporate Partnership Program, 20 Park Plaza, #330,
Boston, MA 02116.

Naisbitt Group, 1101 30th Street, NW, Washington, DC 20007.

Naropa Institute, 2130 Arapahoe, Boulder, CO 80302.

National Association of Legal Services to Alternative Schools, P.O. Box
2823, Santa Fe, NM 87501.

National Indian Youth Council, 318 Elm Street, SE, Albuquerque, NM
87102.

National Peace Institute Foundation, 110 Maryland Avenue,
Washington, DC 20002.

National Training Laboratories, 1501 Wilson Boulevard, #1000,
Arlington, VA 22209.

National Women's Health Network, 224 Seventh Street, SE,
Washington, DC 20003.

Network Technologies International, Inc., The Arbor Atrium Building, 315 West Huron, Ann Arbor, MI 48103.

Networking 108, Cross Media House, Inc., Metabo Hankyu, Nagatacho, Room 402, 2–17–11, Chiyoda-ku, Tokyo 100, Japan.

Networking Institute, P.O. Box 66, West Newton, MA 02165.

New Alchemy Institute, 237 Hatchville Road, East Falmouth, MA 02536.

New England Commons, P.O. Box L, West Newton, MA 02165.

New England Women Business Owners, 1357 Washington Street, Suite 5, West Newton, MA 02165.

New England Women in the Jewelry Industry, P.O. Box 315, Chestnut Hill, MA 02167.

Nine to Five, National Association of Working Women, 1224 Huron Road, Cleveland, OH 44115.

Pattern Research, P.O. Box 18666, Denver, CO 80218.

Planet Drum Foundation, P.O. Box 31251, San Francisco, CA 94131.

Presbyterian Church (USA), Communications Unit, 475 Riverside Drive, Room 1948, New York, NY 10115.

Prison-Ashram Project, Route 1, Box 201–N, Durham, NC 27705.

RAIN, 3116 North Williams, Portland, OR 97227.

Ramakrishna Vedanta Society, 58 Deerfield Street, Boston, MA 02215.

Resources for Communication, 341 Mark West Station Road, Windsor, CA 95492.

Rocky Mountain Institute, P.O. Box 505, Snow Mass, CO 81654.

Seva Foundation, 108 Spring Lake Drive, Chelsea, MI 48118.

Sierra Club, 930 Polk Street, San Francisco, CA 94109.

Society for General Systems Research, Systems Science Institute, University of Louisville, Louisville, KY 40292.

Society for the Protection of New Hampshire Forests, 54 Portsmouth Street, Concord, NH 03301.

Southern Unity Network for Renewable Energy Projects, 506 E. Bellefonte Avenue, Alexandria, VA 22301.

Southwest Research and Information Center, P.O. Box 4524, Albuquerque, NM 87106.

SRI International, 333 Ravenswood, Menlo Park, CA 94025.

The Source, Source Telecomputing Corporation, 1616 Anderson Road, McLean, VA 22102.

TRANET, P.O. Box 567, Rangeley, ME 04970.

UNICEF, United Nations, 866 UN Plaza, New York, NY 10017.

Union of International Associations, Rue Washington 40, B-1050 Brussels, Belgium.

UNITAR, United Nations, New York, NY 10017.

United Nations Economic and Social Council (ECOSOC), United Nations, New York, NY 10017.

W. L. Gore & Associates, 555 Paper Mill Road, P.O. Box 9329, Newark, DE 19714.

Western Behavioral Sciences Institute, P.O. Box 2029, La Jolla, CA 92038.

Whole Earth Review, 27 Gate Five Road, Sausalito, CA 94965.
Women Against Violence Against Women, 543 North Fairfax Avenue, Los Angeles, CA 90036.
Women USA, 76 Beaver Street, New York, NY 10005.
Women's Action Alliance, 370 Lexington Avenue, #603, New York, NY 10017.
Women's History Research Center, 2325 Oak Street, Berkeley, CA 94708.
Women's Institute for Freedom of the Press, 3306 Ross Place, NW, Washington, DC 20008.
Working on Wife Abuse, c/o Women's Center, 46 Pleasant Street, Cambridge, MA 02139.
World Future Society, 4916 St Elmo Avenue, Bethesda, MD 20814.
Zen Center of Rochester, 7 Arnold Place, Rochester, NY 14607.
Zen Center of San Francisco, 300 Page Street, San Francisco, CA 94102.

Index

Index

190